THE RUSSIANS
AND
THE AMERICANS

OTHER BOOKS BY JULES ARCHER

African Firebrand: Kenyatta of Kenya
Angry Abolitionist: William Lloyd Garrison
Battlefield President: Dwight D. Eisenhower
China in the 20th Century
Chou En-lai
Colossus of Europe: Metternich
Congo
The Dictators
The Executive "Success"
The Extremists: Gadflies of American Society
Famous Young Rebels
Fighting Journalist: Horace Greeley
Front-Line General: Douglas MacArthur
Hawks, Doves, and Eagle
Ho Chi Minh: Lengend of Hanoi
Indian Foe, Indian Friend
Laws That Changed America
Man of Steel: Joseph Stalin
Mao Tse-tung: A Biography
Mexico and the United States
1968: Year of Crisis
Philippines' Fight for Freedom
The Plot to Seize the White House
Red Rebel: Tito of Yugoslavia
Resistance
Revolution in Our Time
Riot! A History of Mob Action in the United States
Science Explorer: Roy Chapman Andrews
Strikes, Bombs, and Bullets: Big Bill Haywood
    and the I.W.W.
Thorn in Our Flesh: Castro's Cuba
They Made a Revolution:1776
Treason in America: Disloyalty versus Dissent
Trotsky: World Revolution
Twentieth-century Caesar: Benito Mussolini
Uneasy Friendship: France and the United States
The Unpopular Ones
Washington vs. Main Street
Watergate: America in Crisis
World Citizen: Woodrow Wilson

THE RUSSIANS AND THE AMERICANS

JULES ARCHER

HAWTHORN BOOKS, INC.
Publishers/New York

Library of Congress Catalog Card Number: 75-222

ISBN: 0-8015-6500-6

1 2 3 4 5 6 7 8 9 10

To our third daughter by marriage
Jan Archer
with warmest affection

CONTENTS

PART V

INTRODUCTION

We think of the Russians as being on the other side of the world, but if we look at a map we find that they're only two miles away—the distance between Siberian Big Diomede Island and Alaskan Little Diomede Island. We are narrowly divided by the Bering Sea and the International Date Line that separates our continents, and today from tomorrow.

In addition to being neighbors geographically, both of us occupy immense, rich land areas, which strongly resemble each other. When Mark Twain visited southern Russia in 1867, he wrote, "To me the place was . . . as like what one sees in the Sierras as if the one were a portrait of the other."

Visiting Odessa, he observed, "I have not felt so much at home for a long time . . . It looked just like an American city . . . a stirring, business look about the streets and the stores; fast walkers. . . . Look up the street or down the street, this way or that, we saw only America! There was not a thing to remind us that we were in Russia."

Supreme Court Justice William O. Douglas also had this strange sensation of déjà vu when visiting the Soviet Union almost a century later. He found that the ranges of southwest Russia "looked very much like the mountains of eastern Washington. . . . And when I reached Siberia, it seemed I was back on the Great Plains, not far from my Minnesota birthplace."

Like Twain, he noted, "I felt at home."

Another American traveler, Mervyn Jones, wrote of the Russian plains in his book, *The Antagonists:* "This unending nothing-in-particular—neither flat nor hilly, neither beautiful nor ugly, neither crowded nor empty—is America all the way from western Pennsylvania out to Colorado."

The similar landscapes we both occupy may have influenced our resemblances as people. There is much about the Russian way of life that strikes responsive chords among Americans, and vice versa—its large scale, its pioneering spirit, its striving for the new and better, its advanced technology, its pride in accomplishment, its warmheartedness, its emphasis on education, science, and the arts, and its compulsive drive to explore outer space.

At the same time we have always been separated by differences in our forms of government—first between a capitalist democracy and monarchy, then between a capitalist democracy and communism. "In spite of this," noted Sir William Hayter, former British ambassador to the Soviet Union in 1970, "the average Russian tends to look on America with a good deal of sympathy. It is, in fact, probably his favorite foreign country, certainly the one in which he takes the most interest."

From earliest times bonds of friendship have flourished between Russians and Americans, despite the changing winds of government relations. President John F. Kennedy observed that while we have fought as allies in two major wars, "almost unique among the major powers, we have never been at war with each other."

From the first the Russians had a practical stake in remaining on cordial terms with the Americans—the need of a common front against the naval might of Great Britain, which sought to limit the power of both.

The Bolshevik revolution in 1917 marked the beginning of serious difficulties between the two governments, primarily because Washington feared the Communist example as a threat to the capitalist system in America and Europe, and because the Soviet government feared American attempts to surround, isolate and overthrow it.

The course of relations between Russians and Americans always developed on two levels—on the official level between governments, and unofficially between the people themselves. Often the two ran in opposing currents.

Although Washington often supported the tsars, liberal Americans sought to help the Russian people against them. Similarly, when Stalin encouraged hostility toward the United States during the cold war, many Russians never accepted the policy, expressing warm feelings toward Americans in private.

After Stalin's death a new spirit of détente brought a program to dismantle the perilous and futile cold war, replacing it with an international good neighbor policy. The two superpowers began talks on nuclear limitation and disarmament, and consulted each other on cooling off war-threatened regions. Important new trade deals and cultural exchanges were negotiated.

Russians and Americans have long exchanged and appreciated each other's ideas. "The things our two peoples have in common are numerous and enjoyable," noted theatrical critic Brooks Atkinson in 1967. "They have borrowed our Mark Twain and Hemingway. We have borrowed their Gogol and Pasternak. They have borrowed our O'Neill and Arthur Miller. We have borrowed their Chekhov and Gorky. They have borrowed our Gershwin.

We have borrowed their Prokofiev. . . . Russians and Americans can still enjoy each other as members of the human race who have worked hard, accomplished much."

Despite the fact that the Soviet Union has become the most important world partner of the United States, most Americans have only a limited and inaccurate knowledge of the history of their long and fascinating relationship with the Russians. This book attempts to correct that imperfect perspective, and to explain the persistent bonds of friendship that unite our two peoples despite the different forms of government that divide us.

The author wishes to express special gratitude to Vladimir Belyakov, information officer of the embassy of the Union of Soviet Socialist Republics, for his invaluable aid in supplying Russian research materials; to the Novosti Press Agency, for photographs and information from the magazine *Soviet Life;* to the National Broadcasting Company, for a copy of their June 18, 1974, TV documentary script "The Russian Connection"; to J. Patrick Wildenberg of the National Archives, Herbert Hoover Presidential Library, for information on Russian war relief; to Leon Karpel, Christine Crouch, Charlotte Wright, and Kathy Collins of the Mid-Hudson Library System; to James Brock of Adriance Library, Poughkeepsie, New York; and to Mary Lou Alm of the Pine Plains, The New York, Library, for their generous help in locating and supplying me with a large number of out-of-print and rare books.

PART I

AMERICANS AND TSARIST RUSSIA 1741-1916

A land bridge once connected our two continents across the Bering Strait. Now submerged in the sea, its mountaintops are the Aleutians. According to the Far Eastern Branch of the USSR Academy of Sciences it was probably crossed some twenty to thirty thousand years ago by Siberian nomads who settled western America. In 1961 Soviet archeologists exploring Russian Kamchatka dug up remnants of Indian wampum necklaces in neolithic dwellings that resembled American Indian wigwams.

Not until the sixteenth century, however, did Russian frontiersmen push east across Siberia. Thousands of army men, merchants, and traders crossed the Urals to seek fortunes in furs, ore, and salt in Russian lands and islands edging the Bering Sea. Possessed by a passion for expansion and exploration, they did not let their lack of navigational knowledge prevent them from putting out to sea in homemade boats.

In 1741 an expedition of two square-riggers, *Saint Peter* and *Saint Paul*, sailed out of Kamchatka under the Russian-sponsored Danish explorer, Vitus Bering, to locate and land on the new continent reported to the east. After weeks of fog-bound wandering, the clouds parted suddenly on July

17 and Bering saw the sunlit mountain peaks of Alaska's Kayak Island.

Exploring the region, he found it teeming with seals, otters, martin, and other fur-bearing animals for which the Chinese were willing to pay handsomely in tea and silks. Bering's discovery brought Russian traders to the new continent in forty-two expeditions between 1745 and 1764. Trading posts sprang up in "Russian America"—the Aleutians and Alaska, an area equal to a fifth of today's continental United States.

Traders appealed to Empress Catherine II to help them develop the new colony. But Catherine the Great was loath to involve her government in the North Pacific, wary of clashing with the powerful maritime forces of Great Britain over the fur trade. "It is for traders to traffic where they please," she said in 1769. "I will furnish no men, ships, or money."

The royalist Catherine was not precisely sympathetic to the outbreak of rebellion in the American colonies, but she blamed King George III for mishandling the problem.

Once rebellion had turned to revolution, Catherine refused to support the British crown. She offended King George by rejecting his request that she furnish twenty thousand cossacks to help crush the impudent Americans. Declaring an "armed neutrality at sea," she refused to acknowledge the right of the British to blockade the colonies, insisting that no country had the right to restrict another's right to buy or sell.

Rumors that she might also be willing to intercede with England to end the American Revolutionary War led the Continental Congress to seek her mediation in 1780. Francis Dana was sent as an envoy, helped to communicate with the French-speaking diplomats at the Russian court by a future president, his fourteen-year-old secretary, John Quincy Adams.

"This is the finest city I have seen in Europe," an impressed Dana wrote from St. Petersburg, "and far surpasses my expectations." He had plenty of time to admire it. Catherine avoided giving him an audience for twenty-seven months, warned by her advisers that it would be imprudent to risk antagonizing King George further, particularly if the Americans should lose.

But there was warm sympathy for the new United States of America among Russia's intellectuals. Aristocrat Alexander Radischev, who spoke and read English, saw in their example an inspiration for freeing the serfs of Russian landlords.

Benjamin Franklin was vastly admired among Russian intellectuals, who read his books in translations. *Poor Richard's Almanack* went through six editions. His scientific accomplishments were so respected that the Moscow newspaper *Vedomosti* predicted he would be "honored as a god in centuries to come."

In Paris as minister to France, Franklin met the brilliant president of the Russian Academy of Sciences, Princess Kekaterina Dashkova, and was so impressed by her erudition that he secured her unanimous election as the first woman member of the American Philosophical Society. She wrote to him soon afterward that he, in turn, had been nominated to the St. Petersburg Academy of Sciences, and had been "accepted to the unanimous applause and pleasure of all."

Following the Revolutionary War, America's naval hero, John Paul Jones, went to France to collect money for naval prizes he had captured and turned over to the French. Catherine decided that the brave commodore was just the man she needed in her navy to fight a war against the Turks.

Her request was relayed by the Russian ambassador in France to the American ambassador, Thomas Jefferson. Hopeful that acceptance might help secure a trade treaty with Russia, Jefferson persuaded Jones to agree. So in 1788 Jones signed aboard the Black Sea fleet as a mercenary, the first American to fight under the Russian flag. He played a major role in a successful war against the Turks.

★ ☆

When Catherine died in 1796, Capt. Nikolai Petrovich Rezanov, a court favorite, persuaded her son, Tsar Paul, to charter the Russian American Company, organized to exploit and monopolize the North Pacific. The company appointed Aleksandr Baranov the first governor of Russian America, with headquarters at New Archangel (Sitka) on the mainland.

Baranov and his men were plagued by endless difficulties—hostile natives, mosquitoes, the dank, dismal climate, and food shortages. Company employees called New Archangel "the end of the world," because it took forever for supplies to arrive from Russia.

Baranov won the respect of the native Americans by learning their dialects, dealing with them as equals, and listening to their grievances. His chief difficulties were with some American vessels which defied his decrees against direct trade with the Indians, bartering firearms and rum for furs.

He had a warm relationship, however, with a number of Boston traders. They went out of their way to bring him needed supplies and also American workers, who helped him build the first seaport in western America. Baranov hired some American skippers to take his furs to Canton as agents. Others bought pelts from him outright in exchange for cargoes of supplies.

In 1801 Tsar Paul, hated as a tyrant, was assassinated, and his son Alexander I assumed the throne. Alexander, twenty-four and idealistic, was determined to establish a just order in Russia, based on the principles of the American and French revolutions. The Russian court became strongly pro-American.

Rezanov persuaded Alexander to make Russia a world trading power, and to cooperate with the Americans in curbing British influence. Expeditions were planned to stake out Russian markets. Alexander named Rezanov his "envoy to the world," with the title of His High Excellency, the Grand Chamberlain.

Sailing with the first expedition, Rezanov visited Baranov in 1803. He revealed Russian plans to expand south along the American seaboard into northern California, which was only weakly held by the Spanish. Two trading posts—one on the Columbia, the other just north of San Francisco—would supply all the food needed for Russian America.

Wintering over in New Archangel, the grand chamberlain, an expert violinist, relieved the monotony by playing duets with clarinetist Ed Parker, a seaman off a Yankee ship. In February food shortages drove Rezanov to lead an expedition up the Columbia, but scurvy compelled him to seek help at the Spanish presidio in San Francisco, where he was able to trade furs for foodstuffs.

In February 1804, when the pirates of Tripoli captured the American frigate *Philadelphia*, sailors taken prisoner were liberated by Russian ships. President Thomas Jefferson wrote a grateful letter to the tsar, adding that he hoped closer ties between their nations would be developed by increased trade. In replying, Alexander expressed his own thanks to Americans for having given the world an outstanding constitution as a model for all just nations to copy.

"I have always cherished a deep respect for your people," he wrote Jefferson, "which has managed to make the most noble use of its independence." Alexander's admiration for the American Constitution was genuine. He ordered the preparation of a Russian constitution which would similarly guarantee civil liberties, and freedom of religion and the press.

But Austria's Prince Metternich—the Kissinger of his day—persuaded the young tsar to abandon it as subversive of all monarchies in Europe, including his own.

Alexander and Jefferson, coming to power simultaneously in March 1801, shared a common foreign policy objective as well as humanitarian impulses. Their bonds of friendship were strengthened by a mutual hostility toward British imperialism. Jefferson hoped that the tsar would help him force the British to respect American rights on the high seas. Alexander hoped that Jefferson would keep the British out of the Northwest, where their naval bases could threaten Siberia.

When James Madison became president in 1809 he appointed John Quincy Adams the first full-fledged U.S. minister to Russia. Adams arrived in St. Petersburg just after the tsar had decided to break with Napoleon. "Our attachment to the United States is obstinate," the tsar's chancellor, Count Nikolai Rumiantsev, told him, "more obstinate than you are aware of." Calling the interests of Russia and the United States "perfectly harmonized," he explained that it was because they "could never in any manner be dangerous to each other."

During the Napoleonic wars against Britain, the French decreed American ships subject to seizure as enemy vessels because they carried contraband goods. Danish privateers seized fifty-two American vessels. When Adams appealed to the tsar, however, Alexander won their release. The tsar also defied Napoleon's demand that American ships in Russian ports be held in quarantine. "It seems you are great favorites here," the French minister to Russia told Adams resentfully. "You have found powerful protection."

In 1811 Russian and American traders intersected each other's lines on the American west coast. Ivan Kuskov led a Russian expedition to Bodega Bay above San Francisco, establishing Fort Ross as a trading post for otter and a food-raising center for Russian America. John Jacob Astor, in turn, set up an American fur trading post at Astoria, the northwest tip of what is now the state of Oregon.

America's powerful attraction for Alexander was weakened when he came under the influence of Baroness Juliana Kruedener, a German-born religious mystic. She convinced him that peace in Europe could only be maintained by a "Holy Alliance" of emperors and kings pledged to Christian precepts.

Formed in 1815, the Alliance kept order by repressing rebel movements wherever republicans sought constitutional government to curb royal powers. Alexander urged President James Monroe to bring the United States into the Alliance to work for such "blessings of peace." But Americans were far more sympathetic to revolutionists than to royalty.

Liberal aristocrats in Russia organized the Decembrist movement to protest Alexander's suppression of political liberties. Peter Kakhovski extolled the American Revolution as a better example for Russians to emulate than the French

Revolution, because it had produced no counterrevolution.

When Capt. Vasili Golovnin led an inspection tour of Russian America in 1819, he was disturbed by the extent to which Astor's fur traders were arming the Indians. He warned the tsar that the traders might be preparing to seize the colony. Alexander barred all foreign ships from approaching the colony's shores. Extending the Russian American Company's boundary south to 51° latitude, he began patrolling the region with three war sloops. Washington was swept by rumors that the Russians were planning to seize San Francisco Bay and force Spain to cede California.

John Quincy Adams, now secretary of state, was also worried that the Holy Alliance powers might invade Latin America to put down revolutions against the Spanish crown. He urged President Monroe to warn off Europe. In 1823 Monroe delivered a speech, written by Adams, to Congress.

"The American continents," Monroe declared, "by the free and independent condition which they have assumed and maintain, are henceforth not to be considered as subjects for future colonization by any European powers."

The "Monroe Doctrine" had been born.

Adams informed the Russian minister in Washington that in the American view, all colonial establishments were doomed to collapse as immoral. When this was reported to Alexander, he ordered Adams informed that the Holy Alliance considered republicanism an "expiring" form of government.

Adams angrily instructed the American minister in St. Petersburg, "There can, perhaps, be no better time for saying, frankly, and explicitly, to the Russian Government that the future peace of the world, and the interest of Russia herself, cannot be promoted by Russian settlements upon any part of the American continent."

Alarmed by this open threat to Russian America, Alexander took a more conciliatory tone. He offered to withdraw the colony's southern border to the parallel of 54° 40′ N., and to concede American trading privileges north of this line for ten years. Mollified, Adams eased Russian apprehension by agreeing that no American settlement would be permitted north of the new border. The risk of conflict faded.

When Alexander I died in 1825, he was succeeded by his twenty-nine-year-old brother Nicholas I, who lacked Alexander's intellect and streak of liberality. The Decembrists sought to mount a palace revolution, raising the cry for a constitution and an end to serfdom. Nikita Muravev drafted a constitution which borrowed heavily from the American document.

Nicholas crushed their revolt ruthlessly. After a secret mass trial, five leaders were hanged. Nicholas learned that 1,578 copies of Alexander's once-proposed version of the constitution still existed in Warsaw. Ordering every copy bought up and brought to Moscow, he had them burned in secret. Under Nicholas it became a capital crime for any Russian to advocate an American-style constitution.

In 1832 President Andrew Jackson named another future president, James Buchanan, as American minister to Moscow.

Buchanan negotiated an important commercial treaty that provided for reciprocal shipping and trade rights, each country granting the other favored nation status, and "maintaining the relations of good understanding which have hitherto so happily subsisted between our countries."

Buchanan was impressed by much of what he saw in Russia. Visiting a school for orphaned children of the poor nobility, he heard little girls in the second and third grades recite pieces in French, German, Russian, and English. When he questioned them about American geography and history, he found the range of their knowledge extraordinary.

On the other hand he found surprising ignorance among some of the nobility. Visiting Prince Ouroussoff in Moscow, he was startled when the princess asked him seriously whether the United States still belonged to England, and whether Americans could speak the English language.

Invited to the annual fête at the Winter Palace, he found it "the strangest spectacle I have ever witnessed." The immense, splendid salons were packed with fifteen thousand Russians of all classes, among whom the tsar moved freely to prove he was not the hated tyrant he was reputed to be.

Nicholas told the American minister that he wished more American travelers would come on the trade ships to visit the Russians and "see them as they really were, and not as they had been represented by their enemies." Buchanan wrote Secretary of State Edward Livingston, "It is evident he places considerable value on the good opinion of the American people."

Responding to the president's curiosity as to what the tsar was like, Buchanan told Jackson that Nicholas was a man of excellent character, a model husband, father, and friend—"but still he is a despot." He added, "The great objection which an American must feel to a residence in this country does not arise from the climate, though that is bad enough. It is because here there is no freedom of the press, no public opinion, and but little political conversation, and that very much guarded." The tsar's regime, Buchanan explained, was "afraid of the contamination of liberty."

Foreign diplomats were used to being spied on by tsarist agents. "Since my arrival in this city," Buchanan reported, "I have not received a single communication . . . which has not been violated. . . . The Post Office American Eagle here is a sorry bird. So notorious is this practice that no person in St. Petersburg attempts either to conceal or deny it."

He came to the conclusion, however, that the Russian masses were too ignorant, superstitious, and passive to be ready for political freedom.

Buchanan's commercial treaty of 1832 did not especially delight Russian American Company officials in the North Pacific. Soon an average of three hundred American whaling ships a year were chasing whales through Russian waters. Known as "hell ships" because of brutal captains and fierce crews, they landed in Russian territory to render whale oil. Stealing fuel, food, and women from the Aleuts and Eskimoes, they left behind them disease and alcoholism. Gov. Ferdinand von Wrangell, an eminent explorer and scientist, finally felt compelled to bar them from the colony's shoreline waters.

Serious financial losses compelled the Russian American Company to retrench in 1841. To shorten their lines of communication, the Russians gave up their trading post north of San Francisco and voluntarily withdrew from California. The desire to avoid clashes with Americans may also have been a factor; a great trek of pioneers and traders was under way to settle Oregon and California.

In that year career diplomat Baron Edouard de Stoeckl

was sent to the Russian legation in Washington. A charming and friendly bachelor of thirty-three, Stoeckl quickly became popular in diplomatic circles. Privately he had qualms about a people devoted to elections which "cause disorders and anarchy," and who seemed eager to fulfill America's "Manifest Destiny" by expanding aggressively in all directions.

Stoeckl's suspicions deepened in 1844 when James Polk ran for the White House on the slogan "Fifty-four forty, or fight!" Polk threatened the British with war if they did not surrender all the west coast territory they held up to the Russian boundary. There was more cause for Russian anxiety in the California gold rush that brought great waves of Americans to California.

"The United States are bound to spread over the whole of North America," Nikolai M. Muravyev, governor general of Siberia, warned the tsar. "Sooner or later we shall have to surrender our North American possessions."

He advised yielding Russian America as not really worth hanging on to. Russia would be wiser, he suggested, to exploit the riches at her back door in the Far East. And it would be safer having a friendly United States at its rear in Siberia than a dangerous naval power like Great Britain.

"If this takes place peacefully," he explained, "we shall gain other advantages from the Americans. Close relations with the United States are important to us, for it seems natural for Russia, if not to own all Asia, at any rate to control the whole Far Eastern coast."

In 1848 European revolution, against which the Holy Alliance had been directed, flamed through the continent, seeking to overturn monarchies everywhere. The tsar's army helped the Austrian Hapsburgs suppress a revolt in Hungary led by Louis Kossuth, who fled to the United

States. Touring the country, Kossuth stirred American indignation. An Illinois congressman, Abraham Lincoln, branded the tsar's intervention as "illegal and unwarrantable interference."

Stoeckl, now Russia's foreign minister to Washington, tried to neutralize this sentiment and involve the United States in Russia's Crimean War against the Turks, British, and French. In 1853 he urged the tsar to hire American privateers to prey on British commerce, and give the United States special tariff concessions if they agreed to run the Anglo-French blockade with supplies for the Russians.

"The Americans will go after anything that has enough money in it," Stoeckl wrote. "They have the ships, they have the men, and they have the daring spirit. The blockading fleet will think twice before firing on the Stars and Stripes. When America was weak she refused to submit to England, and now . . . she is much less likely to do so."

The Hungarian intervention forgotten, American sentiment turned strongly pro-Russian. Senator William Gwin of California won reelection by campaigning on a platform of all-out support for Russia.

In Kentucky a company of 300 riflemen formed and offered their services to the Russian legation. A corps of American surgeons sailed for the Crimea to serve under the tsar's flag. Secretary of State William L. Marcy sent an American squadron to the Baltic to protect "neutral" American ships that were running the Anglo-French blockade.

America's diplomats served as spies for the tsar. Buchanan, now American minister in London, passed along British war secrets he picked up to Marcy, who promptly relayed them to Stoeckl. The American consul in Hawaii tipped off the Russians to an impending Anglo-

French attack on Siberia. A small Russian force at Petropaulovsk was alerted, and beat off the allied fleet's attempted landings.

The grateful tsar told Marcy that he would support American annexation of Hawaii, and offered to open a share of Persian and Manchurian markets to American businessmen.

In the spring of 1855 Secretary of War Jefferson Davis sent three American army officers to Russia to study the Crimean War. One, Capt. George B. McClellan, would later use what he had learned against Davis in the Civil War.

When Russia was defeated, English and French citizens in San Francisco staged a jubilant street celebration. Angry Americans secured a tsarist flag from the Russian consul and marched against the demonstrators, who fled after a brawl.

Weakened by loss of the war, the tsar's ministers held a council to consider a question posed by Finance Minister Knyazherich: "Could we hold Russian America if the British—or the Americans—decided to take it now?"

"In the event of a war with a naval power," admitted Grand Duke Konstantin, chief of the Russian navy, "we would not be able to protect our colonies." The ministers agreed that a voluntary withdrawal of the Russians from the American continent was advisable in the very near future.

★ ☆

A new bond of mutual interest drew Russian and American intellectuals closer together. Those in Russia who deplored the plight of serfs found that they had much in common with Americans who fought slavery. A letter from novelist

Ivan Turgenev appeared in the American abolitionist publication *Liberty Bell* in 1856. Revealing that he had wept reading *Uncle Tom's Cabin*, Turgenev wrote, "The Russian nobleman and the planter of the South can cordially shake hands, the one holding his whip and the other his knout."

They did. Russia's aristocratic diplomats in Washington, large landowners all, were popular with southern slave-owning planters. The American minister in St. Petersburg, a South Carolina planter named Pickens, was equally at home among the serf-holding courtiers of the tsar.

When Nicholas died in 1856, the throne went to his son Alexander II, whom Russian liberals hopefully claimed as one of their own. The editor of the monthly review *Sovremennik*, Nicholas Chernyshevski, sought to inspire him to move toward democracy and abolition of serfdom by writing enthusiastically about such American phenomena as Shays's Rebellion, Jefferson's views on civil liberties, and John Brown's raids.

A different view of Brown's raids was presented to the tsar's foreign minister, Prince Alexander Mikhailovich Gortchakov, by Stoeckl, who wrote that they only proved "how far Puritan fanaticism can go." President Buchanan agreed, telling Congress that the people of the North had no more right to interfere with Southern slavery than with Russian serfdom.

Lincoln, who saw a strong parallel between slaves and serfs, felt that in some respects the tsar was less to blame than "good Americans" who supported slavery and prated about democracy. At least in Russia, he declared, "despotism can be taken pure, and without the base alloy of hypocrisy."

One day before Lincoln took his oath of office, Tsar

Alexander II showed himself a far more daring abolitionist than the new American president. He signed a manifesto setting free twenty million Russian serfs. Thrilled American abolitionists put pressure on Lincoln to follow the tsar's example by striking the fetters from America's four million slaves.

If a despot could liberate an enslaved class in one stroke of a pen, surely a nation pledged to liberty and freedom could do no less? But Lincoln resisted for fear of driving border states out of the Union. He nevertheless felt a new respect for Alexander as a man of high principle. The tsar, in turn, showed that he did not share Stoeckl's southern sympathies. When the Civil War broke out, he instructed Stoeckl to give Lincoln "unequivocal assurance of Russia's sympathy with the Union."

More was involved than just Alexander's detestation of slavery. He had not forgotten that the American government alone had supported Russia during the Crimean War. When Napoleon III proposed that he and Alexander intervene in the Civil War on the side of the South, the tsar refused. Throughout the conflict Russia was the only major European power supporting the Union cause.

Gortchakov informed the new U.S. minister to Russia, Cassius Clay, that the North would be allowed to bring any captured Confederate ships into Russian ports.

To draw the two nations closer together, Gortchakov and Clay worked out an agreement to lay a telegraph cable across the Bering Sea, establishing direct communications between St. Petersburg and San Francisco.

Lincoln wanted to learn what the tsar would do if England and France should intervene to help the South. Clay's successor in St. Petersburg, Simon Cameron, reported that he had been assured Russia's friendship would then be demonstrated in a "decisive manner" which

England and France could not mistake. Gortchakov wrote Lincoln, "Russia, alone, has stood by you from the first, and will continue to stand by you."

Abolitionist pressure, and the need for a clear moral position in world eyes, finally forced Lincoln to issue the Emancipation Proclamation on January 1, 1863. The tsar was not too impressed with the halfhearted decree that freed only the southern slaves, and then just cut them adrift.

"I did more for the Russian serf in giving him land as well as personal liberty," Alexander told American banker Wharton Barker, "than America did for the Negro slave set free. . . . I am at a loss to understand how you Americans could have been so blind as to leave the Negro slave without tools to work out his salvation. . . . Without property of any kind he cannot educate himself and his children."

The bloody rout at Chickamauga on September 20, 1863, deeply depressed the North. At this low point in its fortunes, a surprising event four days later sent Union spirits soaring. Behind Alexander's imperial flagship, *Alexander Nevsky*, a vast Russian naval force unexpectedly sailed into New York Harbor. It was at once seen as fulfillment of the tsar's promise to show his support in a "decisive manner," in response to rumors that the French and British were preparing to attack the Union blockade of Confederate ports.

Northern joy was unsurpassed when a second great Russian fleet anchored in San Francisco Bay shortly afterward. Russian Admiral Lisovski told U.S. Adm. David Farragut that the fleets were in the United States "under sealed orders, to be broken only in a contingency that had not occurred."

The Russians were accorded a wild, enthusiastic welcome
on both coasts. New York, Philadelphia, Baltimore, Boston,
Portland, and San Francisco staged elaborate receptions.
The greatest was in New York, where even the president's
wife boarded a Russian frigate to toast the tsar. Russian
ships fired twenty-one-gun salutes to visiting American
dignitaries as their ships' bands struck up "Yankee Doodle,"
convinced that this was the American national anthem.

Thousands of New Yorkers cheered enthusiastically as the
Russians rode like triumphant conquerors in carriages
escorted by the National Guard in a great parade up
Broadway, through a canyon of fluttering Russian and
American flags. Tiffany and Company turned its whole
building front into a gigantic Russian flag with colored
bolts of cloth.

Great balls and banquets were given in honor of the
dashing Muscovite officers in gold-laced hats. Among those
wined and dined in the most exclusive American homes was
the composer Rimski-Korsakov. At the same time as many
as two thousand Americans a day visited aboard the
Russian fleet.

The social event of the season was a ball on November 5
at the Academy of Music, attended by two thousand of New
York's elite, who paid fifteen dollars a ticket. They cheered
and toasted the tsar as the friend of America and emancipator of the serfs. The Russians toasted the two nations'
traditional friendship, and Lincoln as emancipator of the
slaves.

To show their appreciation, Russian officers reciprocated
with a ball aboard the *Alexander Nevsky*. The flagship bore
huge banners reading "Union Forever," and the decks were
strung with lanterns decorated with American flags.

After over a month of such celebrations in New York, the
fleet left for other cities on the North Atlantic seaboard,

where other Americans were eager to entertain the exotic visitors. They were given dinners in Washington by Seward and Welles, and a reception at the White House when Lincoln recovered from an illness.

On the West Coast, when two Confederate cruisers were reported approaching San Francisco to attack the city, alarmed citizens appealed to Russian Admiral Popov for protection. He at once ordered his officers to prepare for the defense of the city, announcing that "the ships of His Imperial Russian Majesty's Pacific squadron . . . are bound to assist the authorities . . . where friendship is offered."

The threatened attack did not materialize, but Popov endeared himself further by ordering his seamen to help San Franciscans put out a huge, rapidly spreading fire.

Most Americans interpreted the presence of the Russian fleet in American waters for nine months over the winter of 1863–64 in terms of Oliver Wendell Holmes's praise of the tsar "who was our friend when the world was our foe." But Alexander also had Russia's own defenses in mind.

England and France made a halfhearted effort to induce support of a new Polish revolt. During the Crimean War the Russian fleet had been bottled up helplessly by the more powerful British navy. Dispatched to the security of American waters, the tsar's warships would be free to attack the great British merchant fleet if war developed over Poland.

Military strategists nevertheless agreed that Alexander's maneuver did prevent Anglo-French intervention in both the United States and Russia.

England and France made a half-hearted effort to induce Lincoln to join an expression of "world outrage" at the brutal treatment of the Polish rebels by participating in sanctions against the tsar. Lincoln flatly refused.

Clay, once more representing the Union at St. Petersburg, wrote Lincoln approvingly, "It was due from us to be grateful for the past conduct of Russia toward us in our trouble, by a like moral support." He pointed out further that if Russia went down under her enemies, those same enemies would soon "fall upon us."

Stoeckl privately continued to feel disdain for Lincoln as a national leader, and for democracy as a system of government. He greatly admired Americans as a people, however, and wrote Gortchakov, "Nothing is impossible for this extraordinary people, nothing is too difficult for them."

When the North won the Civil War, Stoeckl admitted that he had been wrong in his judgment of Lincoln, and of the ability of democracy to weather the crisis. But that was because nothing was predictable about "this exceptional people." As though to prove him right, only six days after Lee's surrender, Lincoln was assassinated in a theater box.

The news reached Russia as Alexander was mourning the death of his twelve-year-old son and heir. Gortchakov expressed the tsar's double grief. The Russian people spoke through Count Leo Tolstoy, author of the great novel *War and Peace* and champion of the peasantry, to whom Lincoln was a "saint of humanity." Tolstoy said, "Washington was a typical American, Napoleon was a typical Frenchman, but Lincoln was a humanitarian as broad as the world. He was bigger than his country. . . . He loved his enemies as himself."

The unique parallel between Lincoln and Alexander persisted when, one year and one day after Lincoln's assassination, a Russian student tried to assassinate the tsar as he entered his carriage. His shot went wild when a liberated peasant knocked his pistol aside, and the youth was hanged.

Despite the high tide of Russian-American amity, Stoeckl was convinced that the United States would soon seek to annex the Russian colony in North America. As early as 1846 Seward had asserted that Manifest Destiny would inevitably lead Americans to colonize "the icy barriers of the North."

Just before the Civil War Stoeckl had been approached by Sen. William Gwin of California, who had been secretly authorized by President Buchanan to offer the tsar $5 million for Russian America. The war had interrupted negotiations, but now Stoeckl began pressing the tsar to sell it.

Returning to St. Petersburg in 1866, he pointed out to Gortchakov that the colony was just a "breeder of trouble" between Russians and Americans, who could become "dangerous neighbors." The discovery of gold in the Klondike was sending thirty thousand Americans swarming into British Columbia, increasing the danger of clashes between Russians and Americans.

"They have taken California and Oregon," the tsar's brother, Grand Duke Constantine, added, "and sooner or later they will get Russian America. It is inevitable. It cannot be prevented; and it would be better to yield with good grace and cede the territory." Besides, bad management of the Russian American Company had caused heavy losses, and the sale of the colony could add badly needed millions to Russia's treasury.

Furthermore the Canadians were seeking to confederate, which would put the British at Russia's back door in the Pacific. Far better to have the friendly Americans with forts on both sides of the British to keep them in check!

On instructions from the tsar, Stoeckl let Seward know that Russian America was for sale for $10 million. Seward offered half. The tsar sent word to compromise. When Stoeckl called at Seward's house, the secretary of state brushed aside a whist game and insisted they bargain immediately. A price of $7,200,000 was agreed upon, the $200,000 intended to compensate the Russian American Company. A formal treaty, Stoeckl said, could be prepared in the morning.

"Why wait?" demanded the eager Seward. He promptly summoned Charles Sumner, chairman of the Senate Foreign Relations Committee, and called some State Department clerks from their homes. All worked until four in the morning. Then Seward and Stoeckl, bleary-eyed and exhausted, signed the treaty that added 600,000 square miles of territory to the United States, at a cost of two cents an acre. Sumner gave it the name of Alaska, from an Aleut Indian word meaning "great land."

Russians in Alaska were given the choice of becoming American citizens with full privileges, or staying three years as Russians to see how they liked living under a republic.

On October 18, 1867, a formal military ceremony took place at New Archangel, renamed Sitka, which now boasted a cathedral, public gardens, teahouses, a theater in a castle, a college, scientific institutions, and four hospitals.

Its status unclear, Alaska became a U.S. customs district for seventeen years, ten of them under military rule. Americans flocked to the new frontier, which soon grew as unruly and lawless as boom towns of the Wild West. The worst offenders were the American soldiers. The troops even looted the Sitka cathedral. Most of the Russians who had decided to test life under the Americans soon left.

The sale of Alaska was not popular with the Russian

people or press, who expressed shame at having sold so vast a region which had been Russian for well over a century. Religious Russians felt bitter at the government for having abandoned native converts to the Russian church.

There was even greater hostility toward the purchase of "Walrussia" and "Seward's Folly" in the United States. With the opening up of vast western lands for settlement, what was the need of "Johnson's Polar Bear Gardens" far away on the other side of Canada? The press jeered at the "dark deed done by night" by a "daft" secretary of state who had been bilked by the "shrewd Russians." Alaska was "a barren, worthless, God-forsaken region . . . a worthless icebox."

Seward rushed to Capitol Hill to plead for ratification of the treaty, assuring senators that the United States had acquired a treasure-house of fisheries, furs, timber, gold, and other minerals, as well as a great springboard for American trade in the Pacific. But the Senate's reaction was so hostile that even Sumner, who had helped frame the treaty, now urged Seward to withdraw it. Seward refused.

He made a strong emotional appeal stressing Manifest Destiny, patriotism, the American duty to spread democracy, and commercial advantages. The Senate finally ratified the treaty by a slim two votes. But the House, struggling to cut government costs in a postwar economy, was outraged that Seward had committed them to spend so much money without even prior consultation. Seward reminded representatives that the United States owed Russia a debt of gratitude for her support of the Union during the Civil War.

For almost fifteen months a bill to fund payment was blocked. Finally, since Americans had been in possession of Alaska for eight months, the money was reluctantly voted.

The irony of the opposition to Seward's purchase from Russia was underscored a century later by Sen. William Fulbright, who pointed out, "We made one very profitable deal with her when we bought Alaska for $7,200,000, and promptly extracted more than $400,000,000 in gold from its mountains."

After President Richard M. Nixon blundered in 1973 by permitting American wheat to be sold to the Russians for far too low a price, some indignant congressmen demanded that the Russian government sell it back at the price paid.

"Gladly," replied a Soviet spokesman, "if the United States will sell us back Alaska for $7,200,000."

During the 1870s there was a cooling of relationships between the United States and Russia. In 1871 ten thousand Mennonite refugees began arriving from Russia, fleeing a tsarist conscription law that repealed their exemption from military service. Honest and hard-working, they made a highly favorable impression in Canada and the United States, and their exile hurt the image of the tsar.

Then Russian Jews began emigrating to the United States to escape tsarist pogroms. Friction developed when they became naturalized American citizens, then sought to return to Russia on family visits or as business agents. The Russian government ignored their new citizenship, treating them still as Russian nationals. Washington protested, particularly when a Singer Sewing Machine agent, Theodore Rosenstrauss, was detained in Kharkov and forced to work as a laborer.

Although the revolutionary movement in Russia was divided into various groups, Marxist and non-Marxist, all revolutionaries generally shared an admiration for American democracy. Anarchist Michael Bakunin called the United States "the classic land of political liberty." The radical Populists, heirs of the Decembrists, organized the Narodnaya Volya (People's Freedom Party), which cited the United States as its model. They sent clandestine "envoy" Leo Hartmann to New York to seek help from American progressives and radicals.

In 1881 a second attempt to assassinate Alexander succeeded when a member of the revolutionary Nihilists tossed a bomb into his carriage. The U.S. Senate passed a resolution of condolence, the New York State Assembly eulogized Alexander, and the American press noted the striking parallel between the accomplishments and murders of Alexander II and Lincoln, and denounced political assassination. Many Americans tended to confuse all opponents of tsarism with terrorists.

Not all Americans were disturbed by the assassination of Alexander. Radical abolitionist Wendell Phillips declared a few months later that Sam Adams, George Washington, and John Brown were the spiritual ancestors of the Nihilist who struck down the tsar. "The cant of Americans bewailing Russian Nihilism," he added, was "most disgusting."

Defenders of the Nihilists pointed out that while it was reprehensible to employ such violence in a country where people elected their leaders, it was the only way to liberate a nation whose tyrannical monarch had exiled 150,000 political opponents to harsh Siberian prison camps.

Meanwhile the Russian masses were stirring. Alexander III, son of the murdered tsar, grew incensed when Russian Jews organized the country's first trade unions and led strikes against intolerable conditions. Unleashing savage new pogroms, he drove Jewish refugees to the United States in great numbers for the next twenty-five years.

"Our long-established friendliness with Russia has remained unshaken," President Chester A. Arthur told Congress in December 1882. That prompted him to suggest to the Russian government an end to the persecution "which the Hebrew race in that country has lately suffered."

In 1885 George Kennan, an Ohio-born, Russian-speaking surveyor who had traveled in Russia in the 1860s and who was now a correspondent for *Century*, returned to Russia to disprove charges about the extent of political oppression. Recognized as a good friend of Russia, he easily won admission to the prison camps of Siberia. Kennan's long, depressing journey convinced him that he had been wrong.

Over 150,000 liberals, revolutionaries, and terrorists had been forced into wretched exile. He talked personally to over 500. The exiles recognized Kennan's journey as an opportunity to arouse American indignation. They gathered documents and facts for him that shed light on the whole history of political opposition in Russia during the 1870s and 1880s.

When Kennan published his findings in the *Century*, later expanding them into a book, *Siberia and the Exile System*, a wave of antitsarism swept the United States. Kennan fanned it by a series of lectures in major cities, winning the support of leading American intellectuals.

Mark Twain, Kennan, and William Lloyd Garrison were among the founders of a new society, the Friends of Russian Freedom, to help Russian revolutionaries. Translations of the society journal, *Free Russia*, and of Kennan's book were smuggled into Russia, where they brought instant arrest to anyone found possessing them. Kennan himself was expelled when he sought to reenter Russia in 1901.

"The history of the revolutionary movement in Russia," wrote one Russian exile, "will remember with thankfulness the name of George Kennan, whose brilliant and truthful book . . . appeared in the era of our severest government reaction. . . . The official Tsarist lie about the general well-being in Russia received the first crushing blow."

The Friends of Russian Freedom begged President Grover Cleveland to speak out against tsarist persecution. "I am of the opinion," he replied cautiously, "that any statement indicative of my views . . . would be unprofitable."

American public opinion was outraged when Cleveland signed an extradition treaty with the tsar allowing each nation to extradite from the other refugees accused of crimes. Newspaper editorials condemned the treaty as a victory for tsarist despotism, and a cynical betrayal of America's long tradition of political asylum for refugees.

Congress angrily refused to appropriate funds to help the tsar relieve the Russian famine of 1891–92 until he agreed to halt his persecutions. Americans' sympathy for the Russian people themselves, however, led them to raise $77 million privately for carloads of western corn which the Red Cross distributed to Russia's famine victims.

American and Russian troops became combat allies for the first time during the Chinese Boxer Rebellion in 1900. As part of an international army, they marched together to rescue besieged nationals in China's foreign legations. In one battle American marines and Russian troops fought side by side against Boxers who made a surprise attack on their columns.

There was also cooperation between the tsar and the American business community, which was allowed to make direct investments in Russia. Among the American firms that built Russian plants were Baldwin Locomotive Works, Westinghouse, International Harvester, Singer Sewing Machine Company, and the steel companies. When the New York Air Brake Company asked for the tsar's help in breaking a strike by workers in its Russian factories, tsarist police were quick to oblige.

Tsarist pogroms continued to be a sore point in Russian-American relations. In 1903 Tsar Nicholas II unleashed a terrible new massacre of Jews at Kishinev. Financiers August Belmont and John F. Dillon joined lawyer Clarence Darrow, social worker Jane Addams, and other leading Americans in seventy-seven protest rallies held all over the United States.

When educator Andrew Dickson White became the American minister to Russia, Tolstoy convinced him that tsarism was, and always had been, a tyranny. White predicted, "I put on record here the prophecy that this dynasty, if not Nicholas himself, will be punished for it."

Nicholas, meanwhile, was also antagonizing American big business by locking its industrialists out of the rich Manchurian market he controlled. When a Standard Oil executive protested to Theodore Roosevelt in July 1903, the president told Secretary of State John Hay, "I have not the slightest objection to the Russians knowing that I feel thoroughly aroused and irritated at their conduct in Manchuria; that I don't intend to give way."

Irritated by criticism in the American press, the tsar's

official press lashed back, inveighing against American imperialism in Cuba and the Philippines. Yevgenii Pravdin attacked Americans as greedy dollar-worshippers and hypocrites who had exterminated the Indians, excluded the Chinese, and persecuted blacks, while piously preaching liberty and self-determination to other peoples of the world.

Roosevelt was secretly pleased when the Japanese launched a surprise attack on the Russian fleet off Port Arthur on February 8, 1904. He prepared to go to Japan's assistance if Russia interfered with American vessels trading with Japan, but the tsar made no such tactical blunder.

Tokyo secured a quick victory, but at a heavy cost in blood and treasure. Both sides desperately needed peace.

Roosevelt was startled by Japan's unexpected display of military power. Hoping to end the war on terms that would keep a balance of power in the Far East, he sent envoys to St. Petersburg and Tokyo to offer his services as mediator. The tsar was privately advised to sue for peace, and promised that Roosevelt would get Russia reasonable terms.

"Only the blind and deaf," warned the conservative *Novoye Vremya*, "can doubt that America unites with Japan to dominate in Asia." But the tsar accepted the president's arbitration. The liberal *Novosti* observed, "The proposal made by Roosevelt was accepted mainly in order to crush the rebellious internal movement provoked by the unpopular war."

A summertime peace conference was held aboard the presidential yacht *Mayflower* at Portsmouth, New Hampshire. Keeping his word, Roosevelt won a settlement, signed on September 5, 1905, that was far more moderate than Japan's demands as victor.

"'While Russia's triumph would have been a blow to civilization," he wrote, "her destruction as an eastern

Asiatic Power would also in my opinion be unfortunate." In 1906 he was awarded the Nobel Peace Prize for his efforts.

George Kennan visited Japan in 1904 with the idea of proselytizing Russian prisoners. The Japanese minister of war allowed him to distribute his anti-tsarist works among the prisoners, aided by a delegate from the American Friends of Russian Freedom. In some measure Kennan was responsible for the 1905 Russian Revolution that ensued.

"Of the seventy thousand prisoners in Japan," he wrote, "at least fifty thousand went back to Russia with new ideas of government. . . . All of them had become liberals and three-fourths of them revolutionists." The tsarist press bitterly blamed the American government for Kennan's agitation.

The tsar tried to divert Russian wrath at the disastrous war with Japan by making Jews the scapegoats. When a general strike turned into revolution, the tsar suppressed it ruthlessly. New pogroms by his "Black Hundreds" sent fresh shiploads of refugees fleeing to America at the rate of ninety thousand a year.

From the Revolution of 1905 to the outbreak of World War I, the Russian government sought to industrialize heavily, using the United States as its model. State Council member Ivan Ozerov wrote a book called *What America Teaches Us*, pointing out that only an American-style public school system could develop the initiative, inventiveness, and drive that characterized entrepreneurs in the United States.

"Look at how much the United States spends on schools and education," he exhorted, adding, "We have to learn from America how to support a . . . democratized culture that seeps into every pore of the people's life, including the lower strata."

American businessmen were less interested in Manchuria as more and more American exports found a profitable market in Russia itself. In 1910 alone the tsar's mills used $50 million worth of American cotton. But Jacob H. Schiff, Jewish head of the banking house of Kuhn, Loeb and Company, led a movement to cancel Buchanan's commercial treaty of 1832 until the tsar agreed to issue visas for naturalized Russian Jews who sought to return to Russia for business or family reasons.

When an influential National Citizens Committee for Abrogation was formed in December 1911, it was addressed by Gov. Woodrow Wilson of New Jersey. Wilson insisted that the treaty must be set aside until the tsar relented. Ten days later Congress abrogated the treaty, and the United States recalled its ambassador for two years.

Abrogation presented no serious problem for American big business interests with a large stake in Russian-American trade. Commercial shipments were simply rerouted to Russia through third countries. And the House of Morgan stepped up direct investments. More and more American-owned factories opened in Russia, selling their goods directly to the Russians with savings in labor costs, transportation, and time.

Bolshevik leader Vladimir Lenin, exiled in Vienna, noted the vast growth of American capitalism with something like admiration. "The United States," he wrote in 1913, "is one of the most advanced countries of present-day capitalism. . . . America is also unrivalled in its . . . advanced technique, the last word in science . . . in its political freedom and in the cultural level of the masses of the population. The ideal of our bourgeois civilization is in many respects indebted to this country."

At the same time he praised the class struggle in America,

noting with satisfaction that Eugene Debs's Socialist weekly, *Appeal to Reason*, had reached a circulation of one million, despite all attempts to suppress it. That showed, Lenin declared, "what kind of revolt is approaching in America." He compared the oppression of the peasantry in tsarist Russia to the plight of the black masses in the United States.

Lenin's studies of the race problem in America were based on the writings of Dr. William Du Bois, the American black leader who criticized the Socialists for not joining the black struggle to end racism. Lenin called the plight of blacks in America "unworthy of a civilized country. . . . Shame on America!"

In 1914, when Russia joined Britain and France in a war against Germany, President Wilson sought to keep the American government carefully neutral. But he did nothing to stop the House of Morgan from floating loans of billions to the British and Russians for purchasing American war supplies. By 1916, however, Wilson was worried over the possibility of a German victory; Russia, on the edge of famine and collapse, might have to pull out of the war. The Morgan interests formed the American-Russian Chamber of Commerce, consisting of over one hundred major American firms, to protect American investments in, and trade with, Russia.

Russian exile Leon Trotsky, expelled from one European country after another as a dangerous revolutionary, arrived in the United States on a rainy January 26, 1917. Other Russian exiles found him an eighteen-dollar-a-month apartment in Manhattan, where he was fascinated by such unique luxuries as a telephone, electric lights, gas stove, private bath, elevator, and garbage chute. "New York impressed me tremendously," he declared, "because, more than any other city in the world, it is the fullest expression of our modern age."

He wrote for the radical Russian language daily, *New World,* and lectured in Russian and German to immigrant audiences. Studying American economics in the New York Public Library, he became convinced that the United States would have to enter the war to protect its enormous investments and markets.

Trotsky and the Russian emigrés in New York City were electrified in March 1917 when the Kerensky Revolution forced the tsar to abdicate. A new bourgeois provisional government took power, supported by Mensheviks who believed in a democratic revolution, as against Bolshevik insistence upon a dictatorship of the proletariat. The new government permitted all political exiles to return to Russia. Trotsky's New York supporters held a rally to raise funds so that he could rush back to Petrograd (formerly called St. Petersburg) and help direct the revolution.

John Reed, a radical young newsman who had visited Russia in 1915, and Lincoln Steffens, America's leading investigative journalist, sped to Russia to cover developing events. Steffens reported that it was not the propaganda of radicals that had overthrown the tsar, but the blind intransigence of his regime in ignoring pleas of the populace for bread.

Reed grew increasingly convinced that Kerensky's government could not last. Rich Russians still patronized concerts and gambling rooms while lines of the hungry poor in back streets grew longer. And there were more and more wholesale desertions of Russian troops from the front.

Wilson, however, was delighted with the Kerensky

Revolution, referring to the "wonderful and heartening things that have been happening in the last few weeks in Russia." The Allies could now be supported as a league of entirely democratic nations against the autocratic kaiser. Wilson recognized the Kerensky regime immediately, and offered a $325 million loan to keep it viable.

The timing of the Kerensky Revolution was perfect from an American standpoint, because it enabled Wilson to tell Congress and the world in his war message of April 2, 1917, that Russia was now "a fit partner for a league of honor." The president was convinced that the Russian people, who had been "always in fact democratic at heart," would now fight all the harder on the side of the Allies because they would be fighting for themselves, and not for a tsar.

Four days later the United States entered the war "to make the world safe for democracy." Next day political commentator Walter Lippmann wrote in the *New Republic*, "Democracy is infectious—the entrance of the Russian and American democracies is sure to be a stimulus to democrats everywhere. . . . The war which started as a clash of empires in the Balkans will dissolve into democratic revolution the world over."

But Steffens reported that Russian troops were fraternizing with German soldiers at the front. Kerensky would have difficulty in pursuing the war, he observed, especially with shortages of supplies, food, clothing, and ammunition. Steffens also wrote that Kerensky's continuation in power was by no means assured. The Revolution "is not all over yet. There are intense issues to be fought out and the fight is on."

After watching worker delegates at the All-Russian Soviet in Petrograd, Steffens pointed out to the American ambassador, David R. Francis, *"There* is the real thing . . . where you should send your observers for information and for liaison." But Francis had no use for the "red mob."

Steffens was impressed with the delegates who debated, ate, cooked, and slept in the great hall of the Soviet. "The first law passed by that representative, stinking mass," he reported ironically, "put them ahead of our clean, civilized leading nations. It was against capital punishment. . . . And the second law was against war and empire."

Ambassador Francis refused to recognize that the Soviet reflected the overwhelming Russian sentiment for a separate peace with Germany. He turned a deaf ear to Steffens's warning that Kerensky must either heed this sentiment or be swept out of office. While they were arguing in the American embassy, Lenin led a demonstration there to protest the death sentence imposed on labor leader Tom Mooney for allegedly bombing a Preparedness Day parade in San Francisco.

Francis not only refused to see Lenin, but pressured the Provisional Government to arrest and execute him as a traitor for opposing the war. Lenin fled to Finland.

The House of Morgan, concerned about its Russian investments and its huge loans tied up in the fate of the war, had a staunch friend in the American ambassador, himself a banker. Francis was determined to keep Russia in the war. Afterwards the loans could be used as levers to exploit the country's vast mineral resources and immense water power, building a huge railway network to carry off its wealth.

But Steffens finally compelled Francis and Kerensky to admit that the Russian people were fed up with fighting in a war the Soviet charged was being fought for imperialist spoils. He was induced to return home to see Wilson and explain the situation. Worried, the president decided to send a fact-finding commission to Russia.

To head it Wilson chose ultraconservative Wall Street lawyer Elihu Root, selected in order to unite big business support behind Kerensky. When American Socialists protested the choice of Root, AFL president Samuel Gompers denounced them as traitors for seeking to undermine the Root Commission's effort to keep the Russians in the war.

Commission member Charles Russell, a prowar Socialist, warned Root on the voyage to Petrograd, "The men whom we most have to fear are the radicals who are called the Reds." He added, "Russian Jews from New York are on their way to make us trouble." Reaching Petrograd, Russell lost no time in addressing a meeting of the Soviet, declaring that American workers were convinced Socialism could be built only through victory over Germany. He was challenged by some Russian Socialists who had returned from the United States. Denouncing him as a "lackey" of America's "imperialistic highwaymen," they revealed that Russell had been expelled by the Socialist party.

Although the Root mission was allegedly only to examine conditions in Russia and find out what the United States could do to help, for six weeks the five commissioners traveled around the country as a propaganda agency, seeking to whip up support for the Kerensky regime and continuation of the war.

Kerensky told the American commissioners gloomily that conditions in the country were desperate, and that it would not be easy to convince the people to persevere in the war.

"No fight, no loan," Root told him crisply.

Russian journalist V. Kerzhentsev wrote in the Gorkyedited review, *Letopis,* "The name of Root was enough to eliminate all doubts about the nature and purposes of the delegation. . . . [He is] known in all Russia in connection with his attempts to help the Russian autocracy close the doors of the United States to Russian political emigrants, and to extradite . . . those persons who had found asylum in the United States."

The Root Commission returned home with assurances to Congress and the American people that the Russians were now staunch democratic war allies who would fight on until victory. But when Dr. Frank C. Billings was selected to head a new Red Cross mission to Russia, Root privately warned him that unless the "bread problem in Petrograd" could be solved, it would lead to the collapse of the Kerensky regime and total Russian withdrawal from the war.

The Red Cross Commission was made possible by a million-dollar donation by Col. William Boyce Thompson, a wealthy mining magnate. Chosen as the commission's field representative in Russia was a unique American millionaire, Col. Ray Robins, ex-coal miner, ex-gold prospector, ex-minister, and a lifetime crusader for humanitarian causes.

Thompson gave Robins the task of getting food, medicine, and clothing distributed around Russia, at the same time campaigning vigorously among soldiers and workmen to keep Russia in the war. Thompson warned, "If we fail, you get shot."

"If I get shot," Robins replied dryly, "you get hung."

Thompson's huge gift of condensed milk, distributed by Robins, helped save the lives of many Russian children in the harsh winter of 1917–18. Robins's travels around the country convinced him that America was "more popular with the Russian people than any other nation."

Thompson called on Morgan representatives to make additional contributions of food and medicine, warning, "Only the most strenuous efforts on the part of the United States will keep Russia from concluding peace within the next six months."

"As go the breadlines," Robins prophesied, "so goes the Provisional Government." He collaborated with the Mensheviks to maneuver politically against the Bolsheviks, helping them stack a congress called by Trotsky to seize power. The Bolsheviks were defeated in the voting. But Robins warned Thompson, "We're on a volcano. Kerensky's got no power."

Steffens, back in Russia, agreed. He was now convinced that only the Bolsheviks could provide the leadership necessary to bring order out of the prevailing anarchy and mood of desperation.

On November 3, 1917, the Bolsheviks finally won a majority in the Petrograd Soviet. Robins knew that the only chance now to keep Russia in the war was a distribution of land to the peasants. But the Allied military representatives in Petrograd refused to let Kerensky even consider it. "Distribute the land in Russia today," shouted British Gen. Alfred Knox, "and in two years we'll be doing it in England!"

Three days later the Bolsheviks overthrew the Kerensky regime, and made it clear that they would negotiate a withdrawal from the war with the Germans.

PART II

★ ☆

AMERICA AND
UNRECOGNIZED
BOLSHEVIKS
1917-1932

The famous October Revolution erupted at 2:00 P.M. on November 7, 1917—October 25 by the old Russian calendar then in use. In twenty-four hours the Bolsheviks were in complete command of the capital of Russia. When Lenin entered the Soviet to report victory, American correspondent John Reed wrote of the wild enthusiasm that greeted "great Lenin . . . unimpressive but . . . loved and revered as perhaps few leaders in history have been." Reed, now an avowed revolutionary, rose with the delegates to sing the *Internationale*, clenched fist upraised.

Kerensky escaped from the city in an American embassy car put at his disposal by Ambassador Francis. Flying the American flag, it bore him safely through Bolshevik guardposts.

American press opinion divided predictably. The conservative *Outlook* remarked, "It is hard to preserve faith in a people who allow such men as Lenine [sic] and Trotsky to get into power." The liberal *New Republic* declared, "In word, thought and deed Americans should . . . be loyal to the Russian revolution." But it did not specify which one.

Ray Robins promptly engaged Red Guards to protect his

Red Cross supplies of food and medicine. As a result, he reported, he "never lost a pound of anything." A pragmatist, neither shocked nor bewildered, he prepared to cooperate with the Bolsheviks.

Robins was aware that Lenin admired American proficiency. In fact, only one day after the revolution, Lenin appointed Anatoli Lunacharsky the first Soviet commissar of education, telling him, "I attach a great importance to libraries. . . . A lot of good things have been done along this line in America."

Unable to see the busy Lenin, Robins met with Trotsky.

Offering to continue Red Cross aid to the new government, Robins admitted frankly that his motive was to keep Russia in the war as an ally. He bluntly asked for proof that Lenin and Trotsky had not waged their revolution as secret German agents. Trotsky convinced him, then agreed to help Robins get his food and medicine distributed where it was needed. "I won Trotsky," Robins said later, "by . . . not hiding anything."

Leaving Robins in charge, Thompson returned home to try to convince the State Department that the new Soviet government was here to stay and should be dealt with. Robins persuaded Col. William Judson, military chief of the Root mission, to accompany him to discuss recognition with Trotsky. A furious protest by Ambassador Francis brought a cable from Wilson forbidding any further official contacts. Judson was punished by being recalled.

On November 22 Trotsky appealed to the Allies to join the Soviet Union in seeking an armistice with Germany, on the basis of no annexations and no indemnities. Wilson and other Allied leaders ignored the call, refusing to recognize the Bolshevik regime "until it can show some authority from the people." Trotsky's plea made sense to Oswald Garrison Villard, editor of the *Nation*, who praised the peace without victory called for by those "amazing men, Lenin and Trotsky."

Trotsky found another champion in Sen. William E. Borah, who called for American recognition of the USSR in an article in the *New York Times* headlined, "Shall We Abandon Russia?" An American League to Aid and Cooperate with Russia sprang up in the wake of Borah's appeal.

But Wilson could not forgive the Bolsheviks for overturning Kerensky, or for branding Wilson's "war to save democracy" just another imperialist war. "The Russian people have been poisoned by the very same falsehoods that have kept the German people in the dark," he told Congress angrily.

Secretary of State Robert Lansing saw the Bolsheviks as "a direct threat at existing social order in all countries." They had to be overthrown, he insisted, because they substituted class struggle for national patriotism, a doctrine that "might appeal to the average man, who will not perceive the fundamental error."

Francis wrote Lansing, "Yesterday for the first time I began to feel disgust and despair because for six weeks Russia had permitted the Bolsheviks to remain in control." He strongly recommended that the United States support White Russian counterrevolutionary armies beginning to form.

In December the harbor of Seattle, where leaders of the Industrial Workers of the World (IWW) were in jail for leading wartime strikes, saw its first ship flying a red flag, the *Shilka*. Port authorities refused to let the ship dock or the Russians go ashore, charging that they were smuggling in weapons and ammunition to help the IWW launch an American revolution. Fifty police boarded the *Shilka*, searching it fruitlessly. Angry dockworkers compelled the authorities to give the ship a berth, but only two crew members, one of them an interpreter, were permitted ashore.

The two Russians were carried off to an IWW rally of five thousand workers, where they explained the dramatic events in Petrograd. The impressed dockworkers decided to write a letter to "Nikolay Lenin and representatives of the Bolshevik government and through them to the workers of Russia."

Concealed inside a souvenir lifebuoy, it began, "This message will reach you only by courtesy of the seamen of the transport *Shilka*—we have secretly handed them the letter." Describing the prosecution of IWW workers in the United States for opposing the war, it declared, "Your struggle . . . is our struggle, your victory—our victory, and any defeat suffered by you will be a slap in our face."

Wilson was stunned early in December when the Bolsheviks arranged an armistice with the Germans, then published the tsar's copies of secret Allied treaties to prove that both sides were fighting for spoils and plunder. The revelations were a severe blow to Wilson's contention that Allied war aims were noble and idealistic, justifying American participation.

Upset American liberals pressured Wilson to demand that England and France join him in public assurances that the old secret treaties with the tsar were now null and void.

When America's allies refused, Wilson delivered his Fourteen Points speech on January 6, 1918. He spelled out American war goals of worldwide democracy and self-determination for all oppressed minorities, colonies, and overrun nations. To hold the Bolsheviks in the war, he promised a restoration of Russian territory taken by Germany, American aid, and "a sincere welcome into the society of free nations."

Lenin, impressed, told Robins that the Fourteen Points were "a great step ahead toward the peace of the world." Robins was given permission to distribute Wilson's speech all through the USSR and to smuggle it into Germany. Lenin ordered Trotsky to stall negotiations with the Germans, while Robins tried to get Wilson to be specific about his offer.

But Robins's request to the White House for details went unanswered. The Fourteen Points had been an exercise in futility; Wilson knew that he could not speak for England or France, whose war aims remained as imperialistic as Germany's.

John Reed, addressing the Soviet before returning to the United States, promised to describe the Russian Revolution to American workers. Arriving in New York, he was instantly arrested. Although he was released on bail, his papers were seized and held for months. He finally won their release, but popular magazine editors refused to print a word he wrote. He went on a lecture tour, speaking to large crowds despite constant harassment and arrest. Then he wrote his famous book, *Ten Days That Shook the World*.

Wilson appointed Edgar Sisson, a former *Chicago Tribune* editor, as Russian agent for the American government's propaganda agency, the Committee on Public Information. Sisson's mission, backed by a $250,000 budget, was to do all he could to keep Russia in the war. Intensely anti-Soviet, he sought to discredit and overturn the Bolshevik regime by spreading forged documents "proving" Lenin and Trotsky to be German agents. He convinced Ambassador Francis, who reported this "fact" to Washington as another reason to support White Russian armies forming in Siberia.

"If you are going back to America," Lenin told an American writer in Petrograd, Albert Rhys Williams, in

April 1918, "you should start very soon, or the American army will meet you in Siberia. . . . Finance capital wants control of Siberia. And it will send American soldiers to get it."

It was an uncanny prophecy.

★ ☆

Trotsky's conclusion of the Brest-Litovsk peace treaty with the Germans froze American-Soviet relations. Washington ordered the Red Cross unit to return home. Trotsky offered to prevent ratification of the treaty and keep Russia in the war, if Robins could get Wilson to make a prompt, specific pledge of swift Allied economic and military help.

Lenin, Trotsky explained, was willing to delay the meeting of the Soviet to consider ratification for two days. But on March 10 when Lenin asked Robins, "Anything new from your government?", Robins had to admit that there was not.

"You'll hear nothing," Lenin predicted. "Neither the American government, nor any Allied government, will cooperate, even against the Germans, with the workers' and peasants' revolutionary government in Russia."

The USSR ratified the separate peace treaty with the Germans that took the Russians out of the war. Worse from the Allied standpoint, it freed one million German troops for the western front. Defending the treaty, Lenin pointed out that in 1776 the American people had "also entered into 'agreements' with some oppressors against others for the purpose of . . . strengthening those . . . fighting in a revolutionary war."

American opinion was bitterly divided. Many liberals blamed Wilson for not having accepted Trotsky's offer. They defended the treaty as an act of desperation, the only way the Russians could keep from being totally overrun by the powerful German armies. Wilson was also criticized for failing to protest when the French, British, and Japanese began invading Siberia to support the White Russian forces.

The British and French demanded American troops to "help protect Allied military stores on the Siberian and northern coasts of Russia." In actuality, they wanted an American expeditionary force to help them overthrow the Bolshevik regime. Czech troops locked inside Russian lines by the Brest-Litovsk treaty also called upon Washington for aid in getting to Vladivostok, so that they could sail for the western front.

"We are told that . . . we should offend the Bolsheviks if we sent an army into Russia," commented the *New York Times* on June 13, "and we are further told that the Russian masses would misconstrue it and make common cause with the Bolsheviks. . . . It is still the duty of the Allies to intervene and save Russia from herself."

Sixteen days later a small force of American sailors landed in Vladivostok, joining White Russians, Czechs, Japanese, British, and the French in hauling down the flag of the Soviet Republic and raising the banner of the old autocracy.

But Wilson had not yet made up his mind about full participation in an act that he realized had all the earmarks of bald imperialism. He finally agreed to give Britain and France the three infantry battalions they wanted, to operate under British command. At the same time he earnestly disclaimed any intention of interfering in internal Soviet affairs.

About nine thousand American troops were dispatched to Vladivostok. Japan poured in seventy-three thousand men. Together they took over the railway line as far inland as Lake Baikal. Meanwhile the House of Morgan supplied funds to White House Adm. Alexander Kolchak for weapons, ammunition, locomotives, and other materiel.

The IWW held a protest rally in Seattle, demanding that Wilson withdraw the American troops from Siberia and recognize the Soviet Union. A copy of the resolution was sent to Lenin. On August 22, 1918, *Pravda* published Lenin's "Letter to American Workers," a response to the IWW letter brought to him earlier by the crew of the *Shilka*. Copies of Lenin's reply were smuggled into New York City, where John Reed helped get it published in a number of Socialist magazines.

Lenin's open letter inspired American sympathizers to launch a "Hands Off Russia" movement. A League of Socialist Propaganda organized a campaign to recruit American volunteers to fight in the Red Army. Seattle dockworkers held up a supply ship for the White Russian counterrevolutionaries for three weeks, refusing to load fifty truckloads of military supplies and equipment. The Central Labor Council of Seattle opened a Bureau of Russian Information.

Lenin's letter also led to a split in the American Socialist party. Convinced that bolshevism was now the only correct path to socialism, its most radical members broke away to form a new Workers (Communist) party.

U.S. troops landing at Archangel were quickly snatched out of American control by the British command in Siberia. They were sent south by train to join British and French forces standing off a Bolshevik attack against the White Armies in northern Russia. An advanced American detachment sent from the Philippines to Vladivostok was deceived into taking part in another action against Bolshevik forces by a Japanese general, who led the Americans to believe that the Red Army troops were German prisoners of war rearmed by the Russians.

Secretary of War William M. Garrison dispatched Gen. William S. Graves to Siberia to take charge of the confused American expedition. The only instructions he gave Graves were: "Watch your step. You will be walking on eggs loaded with dynamite." When Graves arrived at Vladivostok, he was upset to find American troops there convinced that their mission was to crush bolshevism. He dressed down one officer who had arrested a Russian just because he was a Bolshevik.

"Whoever gave you those orders made them up himself," Graves told him sharply. "The United States is not at war with the Bolsheviks. . . . You are only to arrest those who attack you. The United States is only fighting the Bolsheviki when the American troops are attacked by an armed force."

But it was undeclared warfare, just the same. Col. John Cudahy, an American field officer, reported, "In the province of Archangel, on six scattered battlefronts, American soldiers, under British command, were 'standing to' behind snow trenches and improvised barricades while soldiers of the Soviet cause crashed Pom Pom projectiles at them and shook them with high explosives and shrapnel, blasted them with machineguns, and sniped at any reckless head that showed from cover. . . . There seems to be among the troops a very indistinct idea of what we are fighting for here."

Trotsky himself directed one offensive against a village defended by British and American troops, who held out for four days of bitter fighting against Soviet infantrymen struggling through waist-deep snow.

Some new American troops were sent to guard coal mines near Vladivostok, and took military action to keep them open when the miners went on strike. Filled with horrendous tales about the terrible Bolsheviki, the doughboys were baffled to find the whole local Russian population up in arms against the White Russians instead, because of cossack atrocities.

On August 22, 1918, Soviet foreign minister Georgi Chicherin sent an official protest to Washington over the invasion of Siberia. But Chicherin felt that the blame really belonged in London and Paris, which had compelled Wilson to intervene. British and French citizens who fell into Soviet hands were interned, but Chicherin told the politburo, "We have adopted a different attitude with regard to the Americans, to whom measures of retaliation do not apply."

When World War I ended, Americans were bewildered by the retention of U.S. troops in Siberia. Outraged liberals demanded that they be sent home immediately. The *New Republic*, which had originally defended Wilson's decision to send them, now called intervention "a mistake from first to last."

Yet Wilson kept the troops in Siberia for another year and a half, despite protests from even Secretary of War Newton D. Baker. Wilson didn't want to create disunity among the Allies at the Versailles Peace Conference by taking independent action to withdraw U.S. forces from the Allied intervention. The British and French were determined to stay and support Kolchak in his fight to overthrow the Bolsheviks.

"The American people," Lenin wrote, "who set the world an example in waging a revolutionary war against feudal slavery, now find themselves . . . playing the role of hired thugs who, for the benefit of wealthy scoundrels . . . are throttling the Russian Socialist Republic."

The Allies excluded the Russians from Versailles. The American media were stridently anti-Soviet. Mobs of soldiers and sailors attacked pro-Soviet meetings and rallies.

But the "Hands Off Russia" movement persisted. Congressmen began to be flooded with angry letters from the fathers, mothers, and wives of servicemen being kept in Russia.

"I do not know that I rightly understand bolshevikism," Secretary of War Baker told Wilson. "So much of it as I do understand I don't like, but I have a feeling that if the Russians do like it, they are entitled to have it."

Ambassador Francis remained vehemently opposed, and urged Wilson to join Britain and France in sending 100,000 men against Petrograd. French marshal Ferdinand Foch also asked the president to send an American army through Poland and on into Russia. Wilson refused.

But he was far from ready to recognize the new Russia.

As the year 1919 opened, the new Soviet capital at Moscow appointed Ludwig Martens its representative to the United States. When he presented his credentials to the U.S. State Department, they were not acknowledged. Martens tried to take over the Russian embassy in Washington, but Lansing supported the refusal of Kerensky's ambassador to yield it.

Martens retreated to New York City, where he simply opened a business office. When he sought to negotiate trade agreements, the State Department tried to scare off businessmen.

"As the government of the United States has never recognized the Bolshevik regime at Moscow," Lansing said, "it is deemed proper to warn American businessmen that any concessions from the Bolshevik authorities probably would not be recognized as binding on future Russian governments."

During the Red scare that followed the war, the New York State Legislative Committee to Investigate Bolshevism ordered a police raid on Martens's headquarters, and he was taken to City Hall for interrogation. Subsequently Attorney General A. Mitchell Palmer issued a warrant for his arrest, and he was deported with seventy-five other "undesirables" on the S.S. *Stockholm*.

War-weary Allied troops in Siberia grew increasingly disillusioned with the intervention. Mutiny broke out among the French forces, then spread to the British and to Russians conscripted by Kolchak. American soldiers wrote home begging their parents to compel the government to recall them.

In New York the Society of Friends of Russia collected a million signatures on a petition to bring them home. On May Day, 1919, fifty thousand American workers marched through Cleveland with banners proclaiming, "Stop the intervention!" and "Give help to Soviet Russia!"

When House Speaker Champ Clark of Missouri called for the immediate return of all American troops from Russia, he drew resounding applause. In the Senate, Progressive leaders Hiram Johnson, William E. Borah, and Robert La Follette opened an attack on Wilson's Russian policy as "an exhibition of the crassest stupidity." Johnson's resolution to withdraw the troops in Siberia was narrowly defeated on a straight partisan vote.

Years later Senate Foreign Relations Committee chairman William Fulbright observed, "We sent two armed expeditions against [Russia] without provocation. When one recalls the birth of our own nation—that in 1776 our forefathers were regarded as being quite radical, by the rest of the world, as Lenin was in 1920—is it not strange that we should be so harsh toward Russia? Since we have been the most successful revolutionary people in history, why are we so critical of others who follow our example?"

While struggling with a peace treaty at Versailles, Wilson attempted a face-saving compromise to resolve his Russian dilemma. In mid-March 1919 he sent diplomat William C. Bullitt, accompanied by pro-Soviet journalist Lincoln Steffens, on a secret mission to Lenin. They were to propose a truce in the Russian civil war between Bolsheviks and White Russians, both sides meeting with the Allies at Prinkipo, an island near Constantinople, to negotiate a peace settlement.

Lenin agreed to the Prinkipo plan, although not to any cease-fire with the White Russians beforehand. Bullitt asked if he would at least agree to end "Red terrorism."

"Do you mean to tell me," Lenin replied incredulously, "that those men who have just generaled the slaughter of seventeen millions of men, in a purposeless war, are concerned over the few thousand who have been killed in a revolution?"

Nor would he agree to stop Communist propagandists from crossing into Europe if the borders were opened. "Our propagandists will go to Europe and propagandize," he told Steffens, "just as yours will come here and propagandize." But he assured the American emissaries that he sincerely wished "to enter into friendly relations with the great powers."

They worked out arrangements to end the Siberian intervention, raise the Allied blockade of Soviet ports, withdraw all foreign troops, and end the civil war with amnesty granted to all White Russian forces.

While in Moscow, Bullitt and Steffens observed that the new Soviet regime was characterized by an almost puritanical morality, sharply reducing street crime, prostitution, drunkenness, loafing by workers, and mismanagement by officials. They found most Russians enthusiastic about the Bolsheviks, despite widespread famine and disease aggravated by the civil war and the Allied blockade of Soviet ports.

When Bullitt tried to see Wilson at Versailles, he was stunned that Wilson avoided him with an excuse of illness. Had the Prinkipo mission simply been an empty gesture? Bullitt turned to the other Allied leaders, warning, "No real peace can be established in Europe or the world until peace is made with the revolution. This proposal of the Soviet government presents [that] opportunity . . . on a just and reasonable basis."

England and France refused to consider the plan.

Questioned about this later in the House of Commons, British prime minister Lloyd George dismissed the Prinkipo mission as "the personal adventure of two young men." He knew this to be a lie; Wilson had told him of the mission beforehand.

The real reason the Prinkipo plan was sabotaged was that after Bullitt and Steffens had left on their mission, the Allied leaders at Versailles were misled by falsely optimistic reports from the Kolchak forces that they were winning the civil war against the Bolsheviks. Why negotiate at Prinkipo for a small part of Russia when Kolchak could take it all?

★ ☆

Lenin was bitter about the western leaders at Versailles scuttling the peace plan which they, not he, had originated. When the Versailles Treaty set up the League of Nations, he termed it derisively "the League of Bandits."

Wilson defended his Russian policy by declaring on September 6, 1919, "The men who are now measurably in control of the affairs of Russia represent nobody but themselves. . . . They have no mandate from anybody." But on the same day the *New York Times* raised an embarrassing question:

"No one has yet heard any reasonable explanation of why

any American soldiers are in Siberia. . . . If we are not there to fight anybody, but only to protect property, the American people as well as the soldiers will be deeply interested in knowing why. . . . What is 'the job in Siberia,' as the President once called it? Everyone will agree . . . it has not been done; but what is it?"

Walter Lippmann reproached Wilson in November: "The Russian civil war was not a thing for Americans to incite or sustain; blockading people with whom we were not at war was indecent, invading their country without a declaration of war was too much like what we deplored in the Germans."

By the end of the year the president could no longer hide from the truth. Secretary of State Lansing told him bluntly, ". . . The Kolchak Government has utterly collapsed; the armies of the Bolsheviki have advanced into Eastern Siberia, where . . . the people seem to prefer them to the officers of the Kolchak regime. Further, the Bolshevik army is approaching the region where our soldiers are, and . . . if we do not withdraw we shall have to wage war with the Bolsheviki."

With their own troops mutinous, and the people back home thoroughly fed up with war, the Allied leaders were compelled to pull out all their forces. The last American troops left Siberia in April 1920, a year and a half after they had been sent there, still bewildered about the whole mission.

They returned to a strike-torn United States upset by postwar inflation and low wages. The media, cooperating with big business, denounced many strike leaders as Reds, and denounced the Reds in Russia for seizing church property, dividing up private estates, nationalizing factories and banks, and repudiating Tsarist war debts to the United States.

Anti-Communist sentiment grew to a hysterical pitch when bombs were found in post office packages addressed to leading American citizens. Mobs attacked Socialist and IWW offices, beating up and lynching members. Congress gave Attorney General Palmer half a million dollars and a free hand in setting up an antiradical bureau, headed by J. Edgar Hoover, to collect dossiers on every known or suspected radical.

Simultaneous raids in over seventy cities on January 2, 1920, rounded up ten thousand men and women, aliens and citizens alike, most of them union members. Many were given jail sentences of up to fourteen years on the flimsiest charges.

Among those who escaped the dragnet were IWW leader Big Bill Haywood and eight other IWW leaders who fled to Moscow. John Reed, too, shipped out as a stoker bound for Sweden, then made his way to the Soviet capital. Honored by election to the Executive Committee of the Comintern, he died suddenly one week later at the age of thirty-three.

Although Palmer was forced to release the vast majority of those arrested in his illegal raids, 699 were held for deportation to Russia. The first batch of "undesirable" aliens was deported aboard the "Soviet Ark," the S.S. *Buford*.

"We are not afraid of revolutionists," Lenin told a Hearst reporter. "We welcome any citizens whom America thinks dangerous, with the exception, of course, of criminals." Ironically, the roles of the two countries as persecutor and haven for political refugees had been reversed.

Convinced that the war's aftermath would bring world revolution, Lenin established the Comintern, an international organization of Communist parties to coordinate strategy. The move provoked Bainbridge Colby, Wilson's new secretary of state, to declare angrily, "The United States cannot recognize the current leaders of Russia as a government with which friendly relations can be maintained."

When Warren Harding became president in 1921, Lenin appealed to the new administration to establish peaceful relations and trade with the Soviet Union. But the Republicans continued Wilson's quarantine policy, rebuffing all official contacts with the Russians. Postwar depression and widespread unemployment, however, began making both American business and labor anxious to open trade relations with Moscow.

The Harding administration sought to block trade by refusing to let the Russians pay for American goods with gold "stolen" from the tsarist treasury. American firms circumvented this obstacle by doing business with the Russians through other countries, taking payment in gold or raw materials.

In July 1920 the Harding administration felt compelled to lift the economic blockade. American steam locomotives, tank cars, tractors, trucks, and power station equipment began to flow into Baltic Sea ports. "I know of no reason why a socialistic commonwealth like ours cannot do business indefinitely with capitalistic countries," Lenin told *New York World* correspondent Lincoln Eyre. "We don't mind taking capitalist locomotives and farming machinery, so why should they mind taking our socialist . . . flax and platinum?"

By 1921 Lenin had realized that his earlier expectations of world revolution had been naïve, and that capitalist nations were not easily collapsible structures like tsarist Russia. His chief concern now lay in building the Soviet state, if possible with the help of the one great capitalist

67

power that had emerged from the war unscathed and wealthy.

The new flow of much-needed heavy industrial equipment from America enabled Lenin to begin his New Economic Policy (NEP), which permitted some degree of capitalism in order to accelerate Russia's postwar recovery. American businessmen regarded the NEP as a sign that communism had failed, and that the Russians were headed back toward a capitalist economy.

Senator Joseph France, a Maryland Republican who returned from a visit to the Soviet Union in the summer of 1921, commented in a *New York Times* interview, "Russia should be lent money for her immediate needs to buy goods, means of transport, agricultural machinery and other manufactured goods."

Young Dr. Armand Hammer, son of a Russian immigrant, bought a surplus World War I field hospital and ambulance and took them to the Soviet Union as a gift to help the Russians fight famine and a typhus epidemic. At the same time he tried to collect money owed his father's drug company, and to generate business deals on his own.

Traveling through the Urals, Hammer saw the roads clogged with refugees streaming away from the famine area.

"I saw terrible scenes of suffering," he later recalled to NBC correspondent Edwin Newman. "I saw trainloads of people, and at every station they'd carry out the dead. . . . We would hear the wails of little children crying for a crust of bread. . . . I said to one of the officials, 'Why don't you buy grain in America?' We had so much grain that year that we were burning grain. They said, 'Well, we haven't been organized, we have no trade, we're not recognized.' I said, 'How much grain do you need to feed the population of this district until the next harvest?' They said, "A million bushels would take care of the population.' 'Well,' I said, 'I have a million dollars—I'll buy a million bushels of grain for you, and I'll ship it on credit. If each ship that comes over with the grain, you load with something I can sell in America.' "

The deal was struck. Hammer's wheat became the first relief aid for Russia during the famine of 1921. The Russians repaid him with Ural furs, lumber, and precious stones. When Lenin was informed of the deal, he invited Hammer to his office, telling him, "We need businessmen like you."

Lenin showed him a copy of *Scientific American*, running through the pages. "This is what your people have done. This is what progress means: building, inventions, machines, development of mechanical aids to human hands. Russia today is like your country was during the pioneer stage. . . . We're going to grant concessions to foreigners.

"Why don't *you* take the first concession?" he asked.

Hammer replied that he'd seen an asbestos mine in the Urals that he wouldn't mind operating. Lenin promptly awarded him the first Soviet concession granted an American.

Shaking hands warmly in parting, Lenin told Hammer, "Our planet is a small one, and the different countries must learn to live in peace with one another."

When Hammer returned to Moscow, he brought Lenin a gift—the sculpture of a bronze monkey staring at a human skull, both mounted on a copy of Darwin's *Origin of the Species*.

Lenin was intrigued. "If wars continue and people destroy each other," he told Hammer, "perhaps some day only monkeys will be left. And some monkey will pick up a human skull and wonder, 'Where did this come from?' "

Hammer's bronze monkey still sits on Lenin's desk today in a Soviet museum.

Hammer asked Henry Ford for the Russian franchise on all Ford cars and tractors. Ford replied that he intended to wait until the Bolsheviks were overthrown. He would have a long wait, Hammer observed: "They've just given the peasants the land which they hungered for, for centuries. They've given the workers the factories. The people are satisfied now, and I don't think anybody will ever overthrow this government."

"Well," Ford acknowledged, "I think maybe you're right."

He appointed Hammer his agent. Having signed up Ford, Hammer was able to become the Russian agent for another thirty-seven leading American companies.

★ ☆

Herbert Hoover, Harding's secretary of commerce, opposed the economic rehabilitation of Russia as long as the Bolsheviks remained in power. Efficient production, he insisted, "requires the abandonment of their present economic system."

He and Secretary of State Charles Evans Hughes kept Harding from yielding to the arguments of Ray Robins that the best interests of the United States lay in recognizing the Soviet Union, as other nations were doing.

It became impossible, however, to ignore Maxim Gorky's world appeal for foreign aid in July 1921, when a terrible drought produced a Russian famine that took six million lives. Hoover decided to respond to the appeal, as much for pragmatic reasons as for humanitarian ones.

"The food supplies that we wish to take to Russia," he explained, "are all in surplus in the United States, and are without a market in any quarter of the globe." Hoover also saw American food as a weapon, hoping to use it to win the Russian population away from the Bolshevik government.

Ex-Socialist John Spargo, now a government adviser on Russian affairs, drew up plans for an American Relief Administration (ARA). Relief supplies would be placed in the hands of non-Bolshevik Russians, who would thereby "become the most important body functioning in Russia, and to which the people will turn naturally." Such an organization, Spargo pointed out, could become the nucleus of a new government.

Hoover adopted the Spargo plan, which had a number of stipulations. All American prisoners in Russia had to be released at once. Americans had to be in charge of all food stations in Russia, free of Soviet control. ARA workers could not be interfered with in organizing local committees.

American Socialists, aware of what Hoover was up to, denounced the plan, insisting that relief supplies should be given directly to the Soviet authorities for distribution, "without imposing imperialistic and reactionary conditions." The *Washington Herald* agreed, declaring that "the American conscience, the American sense of right and humanity, rebels" against the imposition of political conditions before Americans agreed to feed Russia's starving children from surplus crops. The desperate food shortage, however, gave the Soviet leaders no option but to accept Hoover's offer on his terms.

Congress voted $20 million for Hoover's ARA relief program. Senator Borah pointed out that if the United States could feed the Russians, it also ought to recognize them.

The Spargo plan to politicize relief failed, but the ARA did a magnificent job. Before it was finished, over $66 million had been spent to feed over 11 million men, women, and children from 35,000 relief stations. The

Soviet of People's Commissars, headed by Leo Kamenev, passed a resolution of gratitude, a tribute to the American people.

But soon after the ARA's withdrawal in the summer of 1923, the GPU—Moscow's secret police—arrested hundreds of Russians who had worked on ARA committees, charging them with being counterrevolutionary spies in the pay of Washington. The Moscow foreign office declared that they had been under observation for some time, but arrests had been delayed until the ARA could finish its work.

Hoover was outraged. Walter Duranty, Moscow correspondent for the *New York Times,* wrote later, "At the time I shared his indignation, but . . . there were probably quite a number of the 100,000 Russians employed by the ARA who had abused their position [or] done enough to warrant action by the GPU."

Lenin and the Soviet leaders had more confidence in the goodwill of American labor leaders like Sidney Hillman, head of the Amalgamated Clothing Workers of America. On a trip to Russia in May 1922, Hillman suggested a unique experiment—a cooperative enterprise in which American and Russian workers would jointly operate all Soviet clothing and textile factories under a concession from the USSR. It would "demonstrate to America and American labor the possibility of cooperation with Russia." The Russians promptly agreed.

Hillman organized the Russian-American Industrial Corporation (RAIC), selling stock to those members of his Amalgamated Clothing Workers union "who are interested in Russian industrial reconstruction and wish to help."

Lenin bought two shares himself. Raising over $200,000, RAIC helped modernize Russia's clothing industry and paid back every penny to stockholders who had gambled on the enterprise—with a capitalistic 8 percent interest.

In May 1922 Senator Borah led a new fight for recognition of the Soviet Union against Secretary of State Hughes. Since Russia was a great nation, Borah argued, it would be in the interests of world peace to have her for a friend rather than an enemy, and would benefit Americans through trade and jobs. The United States recognized many nations whose governments had not been elected at the polls. Why not the Soviet Union?

The Hughes forces argued that the USSR disseminated revolutionary propaganda through the Comintern, refused to pay debts incurred by both the Tsarist and Kerensky governments, and had not compensated American owners of Russian property that had been nationalized. For these reasons it did not deserve membership in the family of nations. A Borah supporter pointed out that the American Revolutionists of 1776 had not compensated British owners of confiscated property in the colonies, but that had not prevented British recognition.

As the backbone of its program to industrialize farming, the Soviet Union bought 24,000 Fordson tractors. The first twenty-five to operate in Russia arrived in 1921 at a Black Sea port, and were driven inland in a column by specialists trained at the Ford plant in Detroit. Hillside peasants fled in terror, fearful that the country was being invaded by tanks.

Armand Hammer led the column to a public park in Rostov, where he demonstrated to Soviet officials Anastas Mikoyan and Kliment Voroshilov how the tractors could be used to plow, cut wood, pump water, and pull heavy loads.

When the tractors were distributed to villages, some superstitious peasants called them the "anti-Christ," but after seeing the work they could do, they were hailed as "little brothers of Jesus" and garlanded with wreaths. In Siberia, Tadzhik peasants were so fearful of the strange new machines introduced by the Communists that they shot and killed the driver of the first automobile, and shot out its headlights to blind it. When the Tadzhiks watched the first tractors in action, however, they brought food and wine to feed the engines.

Hundreds of American workers and engineers volunteered to help build the war-ravaged Soviet economy. Lenin welcomed them but warned, "Only those people should come to Russia who are able and willing to suffer consciously the series of hardships inevitably connected with the restoration of industry in a country that was extremely backward and ruined."

Lenin regarded the American agricultural engineer Harold Ware, who was helping him mechanize Russian agriculture, as a human dynamo. Ware not only trained Russian farmers in modern methods, but through the Friends of Soviet Russia recruited agricultural teams to organize state farms. The Americans who came worked from dawn till dark, camping in tents in the field, and coping with all kinds of tractor difficulties—gas shortages, lack of spare parts and water. But they persisted, learned Russian, and taught villagers to operate the tractors. One of their encampments near Toykino is still known today as "the American field."

It was Ware who was responsible for first breaking down peasant resistance to combining their small private plots for collective farming. When peasants begged him to plow their fields, he would get on the tractor and plow a row, but then get off and explain that he could not go further or turn around; the plot was too small. The word spread that the tractors could only be used on large farms. In order to get tractor plowing, many peasants began pooling their land.

Ware and his fellow volunteers quickly won the gratitude and affection of Russian villagers. After a hard day's work helping farmers plow, they would socialize in the evening, singing and dancing with the young people. Ware remained on Soviet farms, developing experimental agricultural programs, for ten years. A modest man, he wrote *Pravda*, "We came in order to teach, but we learned much more ourselves. We know that Russia is strong and patient enough to cope with all the tests and difficulties involved in . . . rehabilitation."

When Ware died back home in 1935, the USSR Ministry of State Farms set up memorial Harold Ware scholarships for students of the agricultural colleges he had founded.

In the summer of 1923 visiting U.S. congressmen found the new Russian society to be orderly, apparently contented, and making economic progress. Although deploring the lack of political freedom, they recommended recognition and trade. Among them was Sen. William King of Utah, who four years earlier had told the Senate, "Any man who supports bolshevism is an enemy to civilization."

Harding began to reconsider recognition, but died suddenly in August. Sen. Burton K. Wheeler of Montana, returning from Moscow, took the matter up with the new president, Calvin Coolidge. Coolidge merely asked, "Is it true that the Russians haven't got religion?" Wheeler replied, "Yes, because for a long time they had too much of the wrong kind."

Ray Robins and Borah also tried to persuade Coolidge. Moscow sent a conciliatory note to Washington expressing willingness to negotiate the matter of war debts. But Secretary of State Hughes firmly rejected the offer without even consulting the president.

Armand Hammer continued to build commercial bridges between the Russians and the Americans. Lenin had written to Joseph Stalin, "I give my special recom-

75

mendation to Armand Hammer. This is a small path leading to the American business world, and it should be used in every possible way."

Hammer's Allied American Company signed contracts with the Soviet Union on behalf of over thirty U.S. firms. Lenin saw to it that the Russian end of these commitments was scrupulously observed, right up to his death on January 21, 1924.

Upon Lenin's death the Soviet government took control of Russia's import-export business, and Armand Hammer lost his agency. But Joseph Stalin and Leon Trotsky, the rivals for Lenin's mantle, were not ungrateful for Hammer's services on behalf of Russian-American relations. They offered him a new Russian concession for himself. He surprised them by asking for a franchise to manufacture lead pencils in the USSR.

"You've announced you're going to teach the Russian people to read and write," he explained, "and you haven't got a pencil factory." When he set one up, it proved so successful that Hammer's pencils supplied not only all of Russia, but also sold in the Far East, Persia, and London.

Alexander Gumberg, a Russian-born American manufacturers' representative, helped the Russians set up the Amtorg Trading Corporation in New York City to handle imports and exports.

Gumberg persuaded Reeve Schley, vice-president of Chase National Bank, to finance the All-Russian Textile Syndicate with a $2 million loan. Within six years the syndicate was arranging all cotton sales and handling a third of all Soviet-American trade. Schley became president of a reorganized American-Russian Chamber of Commerce, which most leading U.S. corporations soon joined. American businessmen saw Stalin's emergence as Lenin's successor over Trotsky as a good omen.

Stalin shared Lenin's admiration for American technology and practicality. "American efficiency," he said in 1924, "is an antidote to [revolutionary] phrasemongering and fanciful invention. It is that indomitable spirit that neither knows nor will be deterred by any obstacle, that pushes on with businesslike perseverance until every barrier has been overcome."

In 1925 American engineers began responding in great numbers to Stalin's invitation to work in the Soviet Union and help industrialize the economy. One of the first was Col. Hugh L. Cooper, engineer of the Muscle Shoals dam, who won Stalin's nod to harness the power of the Dnieper by building Russia's first big modern hydroelectric plant.

American businessmen were reassured about Stalin when he ousted Trotsky during 1926-27. Fearing Trotsky as the apostle of world revolution, they regarded Stalin as more conservative.

Traveling through the Soviet Union in 1926, the editor of the *New York Journal of Commerce* praised its "great capitalistic experiment—perhaps the greatest of modern times."

Nation editor Oswald Garrison Villard also saw the Soviet Union as an experiment, but of a different nature: "Our capitalistic system is breaking down . . . and I feel very strongly that the world is under a strong obligation to the Bolsheviks who essayed the communist experiment." America, he declared, "must view Russia in the spirit of a scientist who pursues the quest of the remedy for cancer."

Many Americans in the arts were equally admiring. Dancer Isadora Duncan declared that she had seen in Russia "the greatest miracle that has happened to humanity for two thousand years." She opened the Isadora Duncan State School in Moscow's Balchova Palace, a barnlike studio in which students froze, and accepted fifty applicants.

Asked to perform herself in the Bolshoi Theatre on the fourth anniversary of the Revolution, she composed a special modern dance she performed to the *Internationale*. She fell in love with and married a young Russian poet, Sergei Esenin, whom she soon divorced. When Lenin died, she stood in line in the snow for hours with the peasants waiting to file past his bier. Composing special dances in his memory, she toured the Soviet Union with them, selling out all performances.

Ultrapatriotic Americans were outraged by pro-Soviet celebrities like Isadora Duncan. An American Defense Society sought to blacklist movie stars Norma Talmadge, Charlie Chaplin, and even Will Rogers as Communists because they had expressed sympathy for the Soviet experiment.

American audiences, however, gave thundering ovations to the Moscow Art Theatre troupe when it toured New York, Washington, Chicago, and other cities. A concert tour by composer Sergei Prokofiev also captivated Americans.

The American scientific community welcomed the world-famous physiologist, Ivan Pavlov, when he visited Rockefeller Institute and other U.S. research centers.

More and more Americans grew curious about the Soviet Union, eager to see for themselves whether it was the heaven its advocates claimed or the hell its detractors insisted.

"GO TO SOVIET RUSSIA," urged an ad by the Amalgamated Bank of New York. "Intellectuals, social workers, professional men and women are welcomed most cordially in Soviet Russia . . . where the world's most gigantic social experiment is being made—amidst a galaxy of picturesque nationalities, wondrous scenery, splendid architecture and exotic civilizations."

Some timid tourists made out their wills before leaving. Many were fascinated by the social programs they observed under the Bolsheviks—free medical care, equality for women, paid vacation benefits at seaside resorts for workers, nurseries for working mothers, legalized abortion, and liberal divorce laws.

When black social scientist William Du Bois visited the USSR in 1926, he wrote, "I have been in Russia something less than two months. . . . I stand in astonishment and wonder at the revelation of Russia that has come to me."

Not all the intellectuals who visited the Soviet Union were carried away with admiration. Columnist Dorothy Thompson spoke for many who, dismayed by the lack of personal freedom and omnipresence of Stalin's secret police, agreed with her that it was a "mental prison" for any intellectual.

At the same time she recognized that it was a frontier society reminiscent of the American West, and held great promise for the future. For some Americans the Soviet experiment was at least an exciting intellectual adventure, in contrast with the dull "normalcy" of the Harding-Coolidge era.

Roger Baldwin, director of the American Civil Liberties Union, took a two-month journey through Russia in 1927. "The fairest test by which to judge the Soviet experiment in relation to 'liberty,' " he concluded, "is not by Western standards of political or civil liberties, but by the effects of the dictatorship's controls and repression on its own avowed object of creating a 'free and classless society,' with the state abolished." In Baldwin's opinion, Stalin's leadership was too repressive; Russians needed more personal freedom.

Novelist Theodore Dreiser also returned from the Soviet Union with mixed feelings, described in his book *Dreiser Looks At Russia*. He admired the Moscow regime for its ascetic idealism, its vision, and its strides toward economic and social justice. But he criticized Stalin's dictatorship, use of terror tactics, and the use of art as a vehicle for propaganda.

Stalin tried to learn English in order to talk to visiting Americans without an interpreter, but gave it up, deciding he was too old. "Besides," he told one American, "I can say in English, 'The restroom is on the left, friends,' which is enough for diplomatic banquets. And I don't need English to understand your wonderful Mickey Mouse movies!"

Meeting with one delegation of American workers, he answered their questions for four solid hours. When the exhausted delegation ended its queries, Stalin asked if *he* might ask *them* questions about America, and did so for two more hours.

"His questions were penetrating and showed considerable knowledge of American conditions," noted correspondent John Gunther, adding, "During this six solid hours of talk, the telephone did not ring once; no secretary was allowed to interrupt."

Stalin's interest in the United States was shared by the Russian man in the street.

"Americans, in particular, were infinitely fascinating to Russians," reported correspondent Eugene Lyons in 1928. "For the older generation nurtured on democratic hopes, America was the land of vast freedoms and individual opportunities. For the younger people, thrilling to the vision of an industrialized future, it was the land of marvelous technique."

Over three hundred prominent American writers, composers, artists, and scientists organized the Society for Cultural Relations with the USSR, headed by William A. Naylson of the Smithsonian Institution. Conductor Leopold Stokowski and Yale professor Jerome Davis were vice-presidents. Despite the absence of diplomatic relations, Dr. James Childs, a Library of Congress official, went to Moscow to sign an agreement to exchange American and Soviet books.

A much broader American cultural influence was exercised by the movies. Correspondent Walter Duranty reported that huge Soviet audiences flocked to see the films of Chaplin, Buster Keaton, and Douglas Fairbanks.

One Russian movie directed by Sergei Eisenstein, *Potemkin*, created a sensation in the United States because of its stunning photography.

As cultural exchanges increased, between 1927 and 1930, Americans saw eighteen Soviet exhibits of film, theater, photography, fine arts, handicrafts, children's arts, press, and public health. American music-lovers were also introduced to the works of leading Soviet composers Dmitri Shostakovich and Sergei Prokofiev.

Visiting the Soviet Union in 1928, American philosopher John Dewey was enthusiastic about Russian experiments in education. He wrote that he had never seen such "happily and intelligently occupied children." Impressed with the Soviet effort to create "a new collective morality," he declared, "I feel as if for the first time I might have some inkling of what may have been the moving spirit of primitive Christianity." One of Dewey's students, Sidney Hook, disagreed; he became a leading American critic of the Soviet Union.

Scientists of both nations, ignoring the lack of recognition between their countries, made frequent contact to consult each other on research findings. Americans were elected to the USSR Academy of Sciences, and Russians were similarly made honorary members of many American societies.

When the Wall Street crash shook the American economy in 1929, Oswald Garrison Villard made another tour of the

USSR for the *Nation.* Contrasting a United States in turmoil with the steady progress of Russia's planned society, he wrote, "The Bolsheviks are working for the good of the masses of the working people." He was impressed by the lack of graft and corruption, noting, "While I cannot approve of a regime that bases itself on violence and force, and is constantly exiling people who do not agree with its economic theories, I am impressed by the vigor and vitality of the government and the unselfishness of the leaders."

As growing millions of unemployed Americans were forced to join lengthening breadlines, many were proselytized by American Communists. President Herbert Hoover's assurances that the return of prosperity was just around the corner sat poorly on empty stomachs. Many of the jobless grew interested in the Soviet Union's planned economy as a possible solution to America's economic collapse.

Stalin saw the worsening depression in the United States as a portent of the world revolution that Marx and Lenin—and Trotsky—had predicted. "When a revolutionary crisis has developed in America," he told a group of visiting American Communists in 1929, "that will be the beginning of the end of all world capitalism." He advised them not to overestimate the strength and stability of American capitalism simply because Americans enjoyed such a high standard of living.

But he was less interested in the downfall of American capitalism than in using its plight to siphon off its skilled technicians. He needed them for his new Five-Year Plan, a crash program to build heavy industry. The plan attracted sixteen thousand American engineers and workers.

Some engineers were imported to revitalize Russia's gold

mining industry, which had been shut down since the Revolution. Stalin, who had read Bret Harte's novels about the California gold rush, hoped that gold would open up Siberia in the same way it had boomed California. U.S. engineers also helped achieve this goal by building an efficient railway system and developing Vladivostok. Within ten years the Soviet Union had a gold output worth $183,000,000 annually.

Some engineers went to Russia for firms like Ford, which had technical-assistance contracts with the USSR. Others were drawn by attractive salaries, especially as hard times worsened in America. Many went because of the adventurous challenge of the "last great undeveloped area in the world."

Engineers from Detroit taught Russians American mass-production techniques. Stalin later told American diplomat Eric Johnston, "The Soviet Union is indebted to Mr. Henry Ford. He helped build our tractor and automobile industries." Stalin revealed that two-thirds of the USSR's biggest industrial enterprises had been built with either American material help or American technical assistance.

Ford construction engineer Jack Calder was appointed chief of all Russian construction, and soon became a Soviet legend. Scorning an office, he rode everywhere in overalls on a baby camel he had adopted, jumping into ditches and climbing up on scaffolding to show Russians how to use tools diligently. Stalin ordered him made the hero of a popular Soviet play called *Tempo*, which glorified Calder as a shining example for Russian technicians and workers.

The engineers, in turn, were greatly impressed by the enthusiastic spirit of Russian workers. Mining engineer Walter A. Rukeyser described "the fanatical pride of all workers from the head director down to the lowliest 'mop' in their factories and their jobs."

Stalin provided the American engineers with every comfort and luxury unavailable to the average Russian, to make up for the rigors of life in the USSR, especially for those whose work isolated them on the new frontier, Siberia.

The Russians were candid about their desire to make over their country in the image of the United States. When correspondent Maurice Hindus tried to see Andrei Zhdanov, then party boss of the twelfth-century market town of Nizhny Novgorod, he was told, "Comrade Zhdanov says he has no time today for an interview with an American journalist, because he is much too busy Americanizing Nizhny Novgorod."

Nearby a Cleveland engineer was building a great new Ford factory. He told correspondent Ella Winter enthusiastically, "I'm building the first Socialist city in the world. We're carving it out of the bare steppes for fifty thousand people." Between 1929 and 1936 Ford's transactions with the Soviet Union amounted to over $40 million.

In 1929 Russian orders were important to the depressed American economy. When the Russian-American Chamber of Commerce organized a special tour of the Soviet Union, ninety-nine leading businessmen signed up promptly. By their return home, U.S. sales to Russia had jumped a full 35 percent.

The USSR was the only major nation to increase purchases from the United States. It was now America's seventh most important customer, buying two-thirds of U.S. exports of farm and metal-working machinery. In the opinion of *Business Week*, it was the Soviet Union that was coming to the rescue of American industry, not the other way around.

This ironic development did not reduce the hostility

expressed toward the USSR by devout American conservatives, who were antagonized by Communist opposition to the Russian Orthodox Church, the former bulwark of tsarism. Priests who resisted Soviet decrees were arrested, and some were executed by Stalin's secret police. The seizure of church treasure, and the proclamation of atheism as official government policy, made American Catholics, especially, bitterly anti-Soviet.

In February 1930 Pope Pius XI issued an appeal for three days of prayer on behalf of the victims of Soviet religious persecution. A widespread anti-Soviet campaign was supported not only by devout American Catholics, but also by many conservative Protestant and Jewish organizations.

A large body of religious American liberals, however, regarded the Russian Orthodox Church as a corrupt organization, unworthy of sympathy. Pointing out that the USSR still permitted church services, they also argued that the Russian social experiment was more truly Christian in its practice of brotherhood than the capitalist nations.

In 1931 Protestant religious leaders visited the Soviet Union to judge for themselves. John Haynes Holmes, pastor of the Community Church of New York, concluded, "Lenin's single-handed achievement marks him as one of the great statesmen of all time." Theologian Reinhold Niebuhr deplored the brutal cost of Stalin's Five-Year Plan in Russian suffering, but added, "Nothing good can be said for the hypocrisy of our world, which uses force covertly for the maintenance of social inequality, and then professes itself horror-stricken by the overt use of force for the maintenance of social equality."

If a choice had to be made, Niebuhr concluded, "an ethical choice . . . would be more favorable to the Russian scheme than our self-deceived western world can realize."

Dr. Harry F. Ward of the Union Theological Seminary

saw the USSR as a temporary dictatorship, but a profoundly moral and cooperative society. He told of being driven through a remote Russian prairie as darkness fell, then suddenly seeing a blinding mass of lights blink on.

"An airport?" he asked the collective farmer who was driving him. "No," replied the driver, "a village."

Lenin had brought electricity to the Russian peasant.

In October 1931 the liberal *Christian Register* observed that many Protestant ministers had returned from the USSR "satisfied that Russia's fundamental principle of a non-profit making and cooperative commonwealth is true to the teachings of Jesus and square with the pretensions and professions of all the churches."

American big business, meanwhile, began increasing pressure on Washington to recognize the Soviet Union. It was hypocritical and absurd, industrialists argued, for the American government to encourage business with Russia, while pretending officially that the USSR didn't exist. The unsuccessful Democratic candidate for president in 1928, Al Smith, shocked fellow Catholics by joining the call for recognition.

But President Hoover remained bitterly anti-Soviet. He encouraged passage of a bill, introduced by Rep. Hamilton Fish of New York, to boycott Russian-American trade as a blow against "the Communist menace." Fish's bill passed in the House, but was defeated in the Senate.

When Amtorg advertised for applicants to work in the Soviet Union, over 100,000 American workers applied for 12,000 jobs. Although Hoover could not supply them with work, he opposed their acceptance of Russian employment.

On August 13, 1931, he acknowledged to a *San Francisco News* reporter that he hoped for the destruction of the Soviet Union—an astonishing public admission for an

American president to make. Stalin could hardly be blamed for being suspicious that the United States, the only major government in the world which still had not recognized the USSR, might be planning a secret attack on the Soviet Union.

Hoover's stubborn refusal to grant recognition, and his openly avowed enmity, may have been a factor in Stalin's decision soon afterward to boycott American products, end all American concessions, and terminate jobs for Americans.

★ ☆

By 1931 as many as ten thousand Americans a year were visiting the Soviet Union to study the Russian experiment. None were Communists, because the Labor Department refused to validate their passports. Intourist, the official Russian travel agency, provided deluxe trains, English-speaking guides, and the best hotel rooms for American visitors. Sixty Lincolns were bought from Ford to whisk them around the cities at a proper "Amerikansky tempo."

"Everything moves here," reported correspondent Louis Fischer. "Life, the air, people are dynamic. . . . I am sometimes carried away and think that nothing is impossible in the Soviet Union."

"People were poor, certainly," wrote Ella Winter, "poorly dressed, living in a single room, short of many things, with the shop windows exhibiting cardboard pictures of meat, vegetables and eggs rather than the real thing. Yet millions of children, workers' children who before had had nothing and could hope for nothing, were eating, singing, dancing, holding hands in the new nursery schools, freed from squalor and disease and neglect. Health and education, literacy and knowledge were replacing the results of centuries of poverty and ignorance. . . . Soviet women were judges, doctors, engineers . . . and were paid the same as men."

She reported a popular anecdote about the arithmetic teacher who asked her class, "If I buy apples for twenty-five rubles and sell them for fifty, what do I get?" And the children chorused in reply, "Three years in jail."

"Russia . . . is the land of hope," wrote Bruce Bliven in the *New Republic.* "It strikes you almost with the force of a blow as soon as you are across the border."

Most Americans who could afford to visit the USSR, however, were appalled by the poor housing, the drab living conditions, the long lines of housewives to buy goods in short supply. They found the Russians friendly, talkative, and full of questions about the United States, which their government had told them they must "overtake and surpass."

Dr. Frankwood Williams tried to get the Russians to show him a mental hygiene clinic. They took him to a kindergarten, rest home, park of culture and rest, puppet theater, school, publishing house, and library, but no mental hygiene clinic. "I grew to understand," Dr. Williams wrote, "that . . . they have set out to create a society that would produce an integrated, adjusted individual. What they were trying to tell me was that their whole country is a mental hygiene clinic."

Enthusiasm for Soviet social reforms led many American liberals to overlook the atrocities Stalin was committing against the kulaks who resisted his program to collectivize agriculture, and against his political opponents. The enormity of Stalin's crimes against segments of the Russian people remained poorly understood until they were denounced by Premier Nikita Khrushchev three years after Stalin's death.

To minimize Russian discontent with hardships under the Five-Year Plan, Stalin emphasized the deficiencies of life under capitalism. The American writers most widely distributed in Russian translation were those who portrayed the dark side of American life—Theodore Dreiser, Upton Sinclair, Richard Wright, Michael Gold, Jack London. Russians were led to empathize with the American working class, but to regard the American government as an instrument of Wall Street.

A widely used school textbook, *The Story of the Great Plan*, by M. Ilin, contrasted the planned production of the Five-Year Plan with the anarchy, waste, exploitation, and economic insecurity fostered by American capitalism. "We increase production," Ilin wrote. "In America they reduce production and increase unemployment. . . . We make what is essential. In America hundreds of factories consume raw materials and power in order to make what is altogether unnecessary."

Translated and renamed *New Russia's Primer*, Ilin's textbook became a best seller in the United States in 1931.

Aware of growing pro-Soviet feeling among Americans embittered by the depression, Stalin encouraged it by expressing pro-American sentiments in interviews with important journalists. He told Emil Ludwig in 1931 that he considered the United States different from other capitalist powers because it had no feudal tradition, no landlord class, no aristocracy.

He reported that Russians returning from America were greatly impressed by its democratic spirit, because they found it impossible to tell highly paid engineers apart from ordinary workers by their clothes. But when Ludwig suggested that Russians seemed to admire *everything* American, Stalin reminded him, "We never forget that the U.S.A. is a capitalist nation."

Within the Soviet Union, the censored government press continued to emphasize American news of unemployment, hunger, criminal shoot-outs, lynchings, bad prison conditions, and other negativistic information to persuade the average Russian that the sacrifices required by the Five-Year Plan, for the sake of a brighter future, were little cause for complaint.

In the United States, similarly, most of the media hewed to Hoover's anti-Communist policy, reporting only the darkest aspects of the Soviet regime to give Americans an unfavorable impression of the Russian system. Even the *New York Times* published at least ten dispatches authoritatively reporting the Soviet Union on the verge of collapse.

As the steadily deepening depression made the need for trade with the Russians more urgent, the American media began to soften their anti-Soviet bias. More and more newspapers and magazines began calling for recognition as long overdue. Some argued that it was essential in order to strengthen the Soviet Union as a buffer against rising Japanese militarism.

The Hoover administration balked, resisting the growing pro-Soviet tide. "I tell you this, Mr. Duranty," Treasury Secretary Ogden Mills assured the *Times* reporter, "the people of this country will never stand for diplomatic relations with a government of atheists and disbelievers."

But a new liberal era was dawning, personified by Gov. Franklin D. Roosevelt of New York, who challenged Hoover for the White House in 1932. Right after Roosevelt's election victory and inauguration, there were straws in the wind to interest Moscow. One of FDR's chief "brain-trusters" was Rexford G. Tugwell, who in 1928 had declared, "Perhaps the time is not far off when we shall, in spite of doctrinaire differences, begin to ask ourselves whether there are not some lessons that even we dominant Americans can learn in the USSR."

William Bullitt and Ray Robins, the team that had sought to persuade Wilson to accept Lenin's Prinkipo plan, were now persona grata at the White House. Bullitt became special assistant to Secretary of State Cordell Hull. Robins promptly took off for the Soviet Union, where he won a quick audience with Stalin. The Russian leader indicated his willingness to negotiate concessions in return for American recognition.

At an international economic conference in London in June 1933, chief Soviet delegate Maxim Litvinov declared that the USSR was ready to place orders worth about one billion dollars with foreign firms. This announcement led James Mooney, vice-president of General Motors, and Thomas Morgan, president of Curtiss-Wright, to increase pressure for recognition of America's biggest buyer of industrial equipment.

Recognition continued to be opposed by the conservative AFL, ultrapatriotic societies like the DAR, and prominent anti-Soviet religious leaders opposed to any action that might "strengthen and encourage Bolshevism."

Roy Howard, now head of the Scripps-Howard newspaper chain, observed, "The menace of Bolshevism in the United States is about as great as the menace of sunstroke in Greenland."

The Defense Department, concerned about the rising threat of Nazi and Japanese militarism, began to think in terms of recognition to win the USSR as a counterweight against Fascist aggression. And there was a strong shift in the national mood, which was now eager for a sharp break with all the policies of three conservative Republican administrations, which had ended in the worst depression Americans had ever known.

President Franklin D. Roosevelt was free to reestablish government relations with the Russians, traditional friends of the American people from the Revolution of 1776 to the Revolution of 1917.

Recognition was an idea whose hour had come.

Thomas Nast caricature of "Old Mother Seward" soothing President Andrew Johnson's itch to be an emperor with the salve of the Alaska Purchase, ridiculed on the wall map as a worthless "fairy land." (*Century*)

HEADQUARTE
AMERICAN NORTH RUSS
EXPED
FOR

John Reed, author of *Ten Days That Shook the World*, addresses Russians at a 1920 meeting in Azerbaidzhan. (*Novosti Press Agency*)

American troops landed in the Soviet north as part of the Siberian intervention of 1918. (*Novosti Press Agency*)

American Relief Administration vehicles in front of a food warehouse during the Soviet famine of 1921–1922. (*Herbert Hoover Presidential Library*)

In 1921 Lenin explained his New Economic Policy to American visitors, hopeful of a U.S. loan. Shown here in his study with an American economist. (*Novosti Press Agency*)

Lenin bought two shares in Sidney Hillman's Russian-American Industrial Corporation, organized to modernize the Soviet clothing industry.

SUBSCRIPTION BLANK

RUSSIAN-AMERICAN INDUSTRIAL CORPORATION
(DELAWARE CORPORATION)

Capital $1,000,000
Shares............$10.00 each

I hereby offer to subscribe for ....*two*........ shares of the capital stock of Russian-American Industrial Corporation at Ten Dollars ($10.00) per share full paid and non-assessable. I understand that my offer is subject to acceptance by the Corporation only at its office, at 31 Union Square, New York City.

Enclosed herewith find $ ....*twenty dollars*........ payment

on ....*two*........ shares. [Note: Subscription for five (5) shares or less, full payment is requested herewith.] I agree to pay any balance in two installments—one-half on or before October 1, 1922, the other half on or before December 1, 1922.

Name ....*Wladimir Oolanoff (Lenin*...

Address ....*Kremlin Moscow*....

Dated ....*2-nd November, 1922*....

(Make all checks, drafts, or money orders payable to the order of the Russian-American Industrial Corporation.)

Member of................................
                    Organization

American engineer Hugh Cooper (left) and a Russian builder working on the first Soviet hydroelectric plant, on the Dnieper, in 1932. (*Novosti Press Agency*)

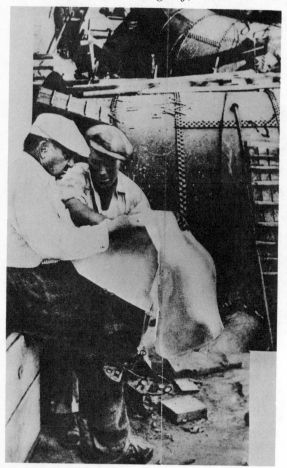

Stalin and Roosevelt at Yalta in February 1945.
(*Novosti Press Agency*)

Soviet and American soldiers met at the Elbe River in Germany on April 23, 1945. (*Novosti Press Agency*)

In February 1945 Churchill, Roosevelt, and Stalin met in the Crimea for the Yalta Conference. (*Novosti Press Agency*)

U.S. Secretary of Health, Education, and Welfare Casper Weinberger (right) at the Soviet Research Institute of Clinical and Experimental Surgery, with his host, USSR Minister of Health Boris Petrovsky, in 1973. (*Novosti Press Agency*)

Marshal Ivan Konev (seated fifth from left) and Gen. Omar Bradley (at his right) celebrated Germany's surrender at a joint staff dinner on May 17, 1945. (*Novosti Press Agency*)

American astronauts tasting Soviet space food at the USSR Cosmonaut Training Center in Stellar Town, in preparation for the 1975 joint U.S.-USSR flight in space. (*Novosti Press Agency*)

Touring the Soviet Union in 1973 with an exhibition of the American modern dance, the José Limón Company return a Russian audience's enthusiastic applause. (*Novosti Press Agency*)

Russian and American scientists of the joint Soviet-American Bering Sea expedition in 1973 study ice hummocks in the Arctic Ocean. (*Novosti Press Agency*)

American educators visit a Soviet school for the hard of hearing in 1973, during the first U.S.-USSR Seminar on the Education of the Handicapped. (*Novosti Press Agency*)

A handicapped Russian child demonstrates her speech prowess to a Minnesota child development specialist in 1973, during the first U.S.-USSR Seminar on the Education of the Handicapped. (*Novosti Press Agency*)

PART III

★ ☆

THE ROOSEVELT-STALIN ERA
1933-1945

Americans who had fought long and hard for U.S. recognition of Soviet Russia—Senator Borah, Ray Robins, William Bullitt, Lincoln Steffens, Alexander Gumberg, Rev. John Haynes Holmes—organized an outpouring of public support for it from college faculties, women's groups, economists, engineers, and church groups.

Roosevelt took office committed to recognizing and dealing with the Soviet Union as an equal, settling differences by amicable compromises. He agreed with Secretary of State Cordell Hull that American-Russian unity was now vital in view of the threat to peace posed by Japan in Asia and Germany in Europe.

In July 1933 the Reconstruction Finance Corporation (RFC) provided a $4 million credit to Amtorg for new purchases of American exports. Then in October FDR sent a message to Moscow inviting a Soviet diplomat to Washington to negotiate diplomatic relations.

The invitation came a few days after Germany had walked out of the League of Nations, sending the stock of American munitions manufacturers soaring. On news of the president's message to Moscow, the same stocks plunged sharply. "There is no doubt that the establishment of official contacts between America and Russia," observed the *Nation*, "will somewhat arrest the Earth's mad rush toward the next war."

On November 7, 1933, Commissar Maxim Litvinov arrived in Washington for negotiations. State Department officials who greeted him at Union Station did not wear top hats, since Litvinov did not represent a government officially recognized by the United States. Ten days later when Litvinov left Washington, the diplomats who saw him off wore top hats.

Moscow appointed Alexander Troyanovsky the first Soviet ambassador to the United States, and Washington appointed William Bullitt the first American ambassador to the USSR.

Recognition was applauded by most of American big business. A jubilant *Dallas News* headline read: RECOGNITION AID TO SALE OF TEXAS COTTON IN RUSSIA. IBM president Thomas B. Watson urged every American, in the interest of good relations, "to refrain from making any criticism of the present form of government adopted by Russia."

Senator Borah enthusiastically wired the president: CONGRATULATIONS STOP IT WAS THE FINE BIG COURAGEOUS THING TO DO.

One of the first fruits of recognition was intensified cultural exchanges. Pianist Artur Rubinstein and singers Marian Anderson and Paul Robeson made concert tours of the Soviet Union. Soviet tenor Ivan Kozlovsky taught Robeson Soviet and Russian folk songs, and Robeson taught him American labor ballads. When they gave a duet program in 1934, huge crowds were unable to get into the packed hall.

Rather than disappoint any of the Russians, Robeson

flung open a window, and he and Kozlovsky performed next to it. Arms around each other, the American and Russian artists sang their songs to the street as well as to the hall.

Pro-American feeling in the Soviet Union blossomed.

Russians began coming to the United States. Some Soviet workers attended American universities to get degrees in engineering. The first Soviet aviators to fly from Moscow to Washington were welcomed by Gen. George C. Marshall.

In 1934 Russian satirists Ilya Ilf and Yevgeny Petrov journeyed through the United States and wrote a book called *Little Golden America*, which enjoyed great popularity in the USSR. Ilf and Petrov were impressed by American businessmen who worked in shirt-sleeves, ran their offices with split-second precision, saw people by appointment, were never late, and never wasted a moment—unlike many Soviet bureaucrats.

Their book captured the vitality and wonder of American life, describing a consumers' paradise glittering with skyscrapers, great highways, cars for workers, drugstores, snack bars and other Western marvels. Despite the usual Soviet criticism of capitalist society, *Little Golden America* did much to increase Russian admiration for the United States.

That admiration was shared by most Russian refugees of the Tsarist pogroms, now naturalized American citizens who referred to their adopted land by an endearing Russian word, *Americhka*—little America. But royalist refugees of the 1917 revolution were far less enthusiastic.

Count Anastase Vonsiatsky, married to a rich American woman, cooperated with agents of Nazi Germany in organizing the Russian National Fascist Revolutionary Party. "Of my countrymen here, thirty thousand want to go back with me to Russia," he told correspondent John Roy Carlson. "I am not American. I don't want to be American."

Anti-Soviet Americans in the United States had the support of politically conservative churchgoers. Years of anti-Bolshevik propaganda had convinced them that all Russian Communists were evil persons. They branded as "Bolshevik lies" all reports indicating that the Russian people in general were better off under Stalin than the tsar.

Equally adamant, many American liberals refused to believe any unpleasant truths about Stalin. They branded as "Red scares" all reports of the millions of kulaks murdered by Stalin for resisting his collectivization program, and of terror tactics used by his secret police against political opponents.

Americans, conditioned to thinking in terms of "good guys and bad guys," lacked the sophistication of the more realistic Europeans, who expected both people and government to be mixtures of good and bad qualities.

Stalin, eyeing the rise of Hitler in Germany apprehensively, brought the Soviet Union into the League of Nations in 1934, urging collective security against the threat of Nazi militarism. Britain and France ignored the Russian plea, secretly favoring an attack by Germany on the Soviet Union, which would weaken both nations, thereby reducing the twin threats of fascism and communism. Roosevelt kept the United States neutral, aware that American sentiment was overwhelmingly in favor of staying out of any more European wars.

Stalin terminated Ford's five-year-old contract in 1934 because the Soviet Union could now make its own cars and tractors. Some American workers were not sorry to come home, because the cost of living for foreigners had become severely inflated, with coffee costing four dollars a pound, butter two dollars a pound, and sugar taxed 85 percent. At the same time the standard of living was improving for Russians themselves.

Following a trip to the United States by Minister of Food Anastas Mikoyan, Russians were introduced to such new treats as cornflakes, tomato juice, and Eskimo Pie, and an automat was opened in Moscow. But the USSR had a long way to go to rival American economic standards, even in the depression of the thirties.

In 1935 the International Federation of Trade Unions conferred with Russian unions about forming a united front against fascism. The AFL was invited to join, but its president, William Green, refused, arguing that the Russian unions were no better than the Nazi labor front in Germany.

Now, as before, the AFL remained stubbornly opposed to labor radicals, whether Russian or American. Gompers and Green were dedicated to cooperation with capitalism, not to replacing it with some form of socialism.

Some important Americans in 1935 were still eager to see the destruction of the Soviet government. FDR was forced to reprimand Rear Adm. Yates Sterling, Jr., for openly calling for a partnership with Hitler in a "great crusade led by Germany . . . not only forever laying the ghost of bolshevism, but for opening up the fertile land of Russia to a crowded and industrially hungry Europe."

Such inflammatory statements hardly helped inspire Soviet trust in the intentions of the American military.

In 1936 Gen. Francisco Franco staged a Fascist revolt against the legally elected, democratic (Loyalist) government of Spain. Britain and France declared a hypocritical policy of nonintervention, ignoring the fact that Franco was being supported by German and Italian bombers, armaments, officers, and fighting units. Roosevelt sympathized with the Loyalists, but at Secretary of State Hull's insistence that any other policy was too dangerous, joined Britain and France in a "neutral" blockade that hurt the Loyalists.

The only two nations to come to the aid of republican Madrid were the Soviet Union and Mexico.

"Russia's help to the Loyalists," observed *Nation* correspondent Louis Fischer, "was in sharp contrast with the stupid, scandalous pro-Franco behavior of the democracies—'Non-intervention' they called it."

Through publisher Roy Howard, Stalin appealed to Americans for a collective security pact against Fascist aggression. He had no plans for world revolution, he assured Howard, and Americans who thought he did were victims of "a tragi-comic misunderstanding." Stalin explained, "The export of revolution is nonsense. Each country makes its own revolution, if it wants to, and if it does not want to, there will be no revolution."

He told Howard, "The Soviet system will not evolve into American democracy, or vice versa. We can peacefully exist side by side if we don't find fault with each other over every trifling matter." His appeal for peaceful coexistence would be echoed later by his successors, Khrushchev and Brezhnev.

When the democracies refused to help Loyalist Spain, Stalin ordered the Comintern to recruit an International Brigade of volunteers to help defend Madrid. A leading organizer of the brigade was Josep Broz Tito of Yugoslavia. Among its several thousand American volunteers were not only Communists, but liberals who saw the Spanish Civil War as the first crucial defense of democracy against Fascist aggression.

They were trained in the Abraham Lincoln Brigade by Soviet military advisers. Their weapons were 1914 Remingtons manufactured for Tsarist Russia, with the tsar's two-headed eagle stamped on the barrels.

The ragged, poorly equipped Loyalist army was no match for the powerful Franco-Hitler-Mussolini forces. Germany and Italy were close, Russia too far away. After almost three years of heroic popular resistance, Spain was lost to fascism. In the struggle 120 Americans were killed, 175 wounded.

Stalin grew increasingly suspicious that the Western powers planned to destroy the Soviet Union by "capitalistic encirclement," using Nazi Germany as their military pawn. His suspicions were deepened by their rejection of a collective security pact against fascism. Still fresh in Stalin's memory was the Allies' intervention in Siberia.

Becoming paranoiac about foreign spies, Stalin arrested many highly placed Soviet officials on charges of plotting with the West against him. His purges drew worldwide criticism, especially in the United States, where Soviet critics cited them as proof that dissent was impossible in Russia.

To offset this criticism, Stalin introduced a new Soviet constitution in 1937, claiming that it provided even greater freedom of speech and press than in the United States, because it turned over the media and the streets to Russian workers and their organizations. But in practice Stalin continued to censor political opposition. When it was suggested to Roosevelt that he counter Stalin's propaganda, he replied dryly that the best answer might simply be to bombard the Russians with several tons of Sears, Roebuck catalogues.

On the twentieth anniversary of the 1917 revolution, Corliss Lamont, chairman of the American-Soviet

Friendship Society, presented to Ambassador Troyanovsky a "Gold Book" of goodwill signed by 100,000 Americans. But millions of Americans were questioning whether something wasn't seriously wrong with a regime that purged so many hundreds of top officials and army officers for treason.

Ambassador Bullitt became hostile to Soviet policy and confided to William E. Dodd, U.S. ambassador to Germany, that he now approved of a French-German alliance against Russia, and that he also favored Japan's seizure of the Siberian peninsula.

Bullitt was replaced in January 1937 by Joseph E. Davies, who attended the public trials for treason Stalin held in Moscow, and reported his observations to Washington. Davies decided that Stalin had four purposes in staging the Moscow trials—to warn all plotters against him; to discredit his old enemy Trotsky, whom he had exiled abroad; to stir patriotic feeling against Germany and Japan; and to prove by public confessions of the accused that his purge was no frame-up, but was based on authentic evidence.

Davies was not convinced that all of those found guilty were guilty. But he reported, "I have talked to many, if not all, of the members of the Diplomatic Corps here, and, with possibly one exception, they are all of the opinion that the proceedings established clearly the existence of a political plot and conspiracy to overthrow the government."

The American ambassador urged FDR not to let controversy over the Moscow trials disturb Russian-American relations.

"The resources of Russia, strategic and necessary in time of war, complement and supply the lack of those existing in the United States," he pointed out. ". . . If Japan should go berserk by any chance, the fact that Russia is at her back door is of consequence to us. The Soviet Union is more friendly to the United States than to any foreign power. . . . Communism holds no serious threat to the United States. Friendly relations in the future may be of great general value."

When Davies left Moscow in June 1938, Soviet President Mikhail Kalinin told him, "We are sorry you are leaving. While you are not in accord with our belief and our political ideology, we believe you to have been honest in your appraisal."

"I came to have a deep respect and affection for the Russian people." Davies wrote in *Mission to Moscow*. "They have great qualities of imagination and idealism which they have reflected in their literature, in their music, and in their art. They have equally great spiritual qualities which they have translated into aspirations to better the conditions of . . . common man."

Most Americans, despite Davies, were shocked by the Moscow trials, which split the intellectual community. Many liberals found it difficult to believe that old Bolsheviks like Radek, Zinoviev, and Bukharin, let alone Trotsky, had been conspiring with Berlin and Tokyo. Confessions at the trial, these critics believed, had been wrung from defendants by brainwashing, torture, or threats to family.

Black congressman Adam Clayton Powell, up to now a staunch defender of Moscow, sighed, "The Soviet Union seems to have gone berserk." Villard's enthusiasm likewise cooled in the *Nation*. American diplomat Charles Bohlen noted, "The purges affected all foreigners in Moscow and especially their relations with the Russian people." Stalin's vendetta against his political opponents lost for the Soviet Union much of the world prestige he had won for it by his aid to Spain.

In London U.S. Ambassador Joseph Kennedy, father of the future president, saw the Soviet Union, not Nazi Germany, as the greatest threat to the United States. He urged the State Department to encourage a free hand for the Nazis in eastern Europe. His thinking was shared by the conservative ministers of Britain and France.

When Hitler threatened Czechoslovakia, they appeased him by signing the Munich Pact that let him take the Czech Sudetenland. Within six months the Nazis had swallowed all of Czechoslovakia, and Nazi tanks stood poised at the borders of Poland. Stalin's suspicions of the Western democracies hardened to grim conviction. They would do nothing to stop Hitler as long as German tank columns were aimed at the Soviet Union. When Russia was attacked, the West would once more stand aside and let fascism triumph, as in Spain.

Stalin moved swiftly. In a surprise move he signed a nonaggression pact with Hitler on August 24, 1939.

When the Nazis attacked Poland, Soviet troops took eastern Poland. The Nazi-Soviet pact stunned the world. No denunciations were more outraged than those of British and French officials who had signed the Munich pact with Hitler.

In Stalin's view, he had bought valuable time to prepare Russian defenses, in case Hitler decided to revert to his original plan to destroy the USSR. But his action shocked American liberals who until then had supported the Soviet Union as the only anti-Fascist world power.

A schism developed in the American League Against War and Fascism. Hard-line Communists insisted that the Nazi-Soviet pact should be supported because it had thwarted the "capitalist plot" to goad Hitler into attacking the Soviet Union. Liberals argued that for Stalin to negotiate with Hitler was a betrayal of antifascism. Disillusioned, over half the membership of the American League dropped out.

American Communist party slogans dutifully echoed the Moscow party line: "Keep America out of the imperialist war!" "Support the peace policy of the Soviet Union!" But the party, too, suffered mass defections by disgruntled comrades.

It was now obvious to the British and French governments that Hitler intended to double-cross them, unleashing his aggression against the West instead of the USSR. England, bound by treaty to go to the aid of the Poles, declared war on Germany and was supported by France. World War II had begun.

★ ☆

Now it was Stalin's turn to stay on the sidelines as the capitalist powers fought among themselves, an ironic turning of the tables. To guard Russia's northern flank against a surprise attack, he demanded that Finland "rectify" the Russo-Finnish border, which was only twenty miles from Leningrad.

When the Finns refused to give up any territory for the Russians to use as a buffer, Stalin sent the Red Army against their border fortifications in December 1939. Smashing the Finns' Mannerheim Line, the Red Army speared into Finland.

Most American newspapers denounced Stalin as a Red equivalent of Hitler. But when the Russians stopped fighting, Secretary of State Hull noted that their mild peace terms to Finland left the Finns independent—"in marked contrast to the results of similar campaigns by Nazi Germany."

American indignation nevertheless remained high because Finland had been the one European nation to pay its World War I debt to the United States. Roosevelt denounced the Russian incursion as a "wanton disregard for law." He ordered Treasury Secretary Henry Morgenthau, Jr., to embargo sales of American aluminum, gas, and other raw materials to the USSR.

Foreign Minister Molotov saw American aid to Britain and France as the forerunner of another world war for imperialist purposes. But now Britain and France, deeply worried about surviving the onslaught of Hitler's powerful war machine, were hopeful that the Soviet Union could be persuaded to become an ally.

British Intelligence learned that Hitler was preparing to double-cross Stalin with a surprise attack on June 22, 1941, the anniversary of Napoleon's invasion of Tsarist Russia. At the end of April, Churchill sent a secret warning to Stalin.

Stalin refused to believe it, suspecting the British of trying to lure him into breaking the Nazi-Soviet pact. Nor did he believe it when American Intelligence also made the same discovery, and Washington notified Moscow.

On June 22, along a 1,500-mile front reaching from Finland to the Black Sea, the Nazis launched an all-out blitzkrieg against Russia, confident of a quick victory.

Overnight the anger and misunderstandings between the Americans and the Russians dissolved. Once more, as in other times of mutual crisis, strong bonds of sympathy were quickly forged between the two nations. At one stroke the USSR had become a war ally of England and France, just as Tsarist Russia had been during World War I.

Roosevelt branded the Nazi armies a serious threat to American security, and pledged every assistance to the embattled Russians. Releasing Soviet assets he had frozen after the invasion of Finland, he made them available to Moscow for arms purchases.

To reduce religious opposition to the Soviet Union, FDR wrote the pope that while Russia and Germany were both dictatorships, "this Russian dictatorship is less dangerous to the safety of other nations . . . to the Church as such, and to humanity in general."

A cold note of dissent was sounded in July 1941 by Sen. Harry S. Truman. As the Nazi armies overran western Russia, he declared, "If we see that Germany is winning the war, we ought to help Russia, and if Russia is winning we ought to help Germany, and in that way let them kill as many as possible." Thus, even at the outset of World War II, the philosophy of the cold war was already enunciated by the American destined to become president in the postwar world.

Even more hostile were Charles Lindbergh and other prominent American isolationists who opposed aid to the Soviet Union. The U.S. War Department predicted that Stalin's forces would be wiped out in eight weeks. Undaunted, FDR sent envoy Harry L. Hopkins to Stalin on July 30 to work out an aid program for the Russians.

In Moscow Stalin told Hopkins, "Give us antiaircraft guns and aluminum, and we can fight for three to four years." A Lend-Lease program was drafted to provide large-scale military aid. Stalin warned Hopkins that the Russians and English alone would have a tough time defeating Hitler. Sooner or later, he said, the Americans would inevitably become Nazi targets, so why didn't they join the Allies now?

"I would welcome American troops on any part of the Russian front," Stalin told Hopkins, "under the complete command of the American army." It was an astonishing offer to the country that had once sent troops to Siberia to help overthrow the Soviet government, but proved again that in a crisis the Russians trusted Americans above any other people.

Hopkins reported to FDR that the strength, ability, and will of the Russians to resist the Nazi onslaught was far greater than most Western military experts perceived.

This became apparent when the Russians were able to hold, and eventually throw back, Hitler's panzer divisions with their own tanks and armored cars, added to those that arrived from America in Lend-Lease ships.

Most Lend-Lease war supplies went to Murmansk in North Sea convoys, which at first were unmolested by the Germans. Soon fierce Nazi air and submarine attacks sank so many ships that FDR and Churchill were forced to suspend the Murmansk run. Irked, Stalin accused them of a breach of faith.

At one point, delays in American supplies were explained to Stalin as the result of strikes holding up production.

"How is that possible?" he snapped incredulously at the American ambassador. "Don't you have police?" American Communists, at one time ardent proponents of strikes, now urged workers to stick to their jobs and double production.

When Pearl Harbor made the United States a full war ally of the Soviet Union, Stalin welcomed the Americans as brothers-in-arms. He urged an Anglo-American attack in the West as quickly as possible, to ease pressure on the embattled Russians by opening up a second front.

Russian-American friendship and goodwill blossomed.

The new flood of American supplies pouring into the Soviet Union led admiring Russians to ask the seamen unloading them, "Things are better in America, aren't they?" Red Army soldiers began using the word

"Studebaker" as a superlative term of praise for attractive young women.

There was an enormous outpouring of affection for Roosevelt. The Russians honored the 450th anniversary of the discovery of America with a series of lectures and exhibits on the United States in leading Soviet cities.

In June 1942 Molotov arrived in Washington incognito as "Mr. Brown," for security reasons. His cover was somewhat blown by an escort of ten motorcycle police. At the White House he explained that Stalin needed assurances of American and British intentions to open a second front that year, to draw off forty Nazi divisions from the Russian front.

Roosevelt gave Molotov those assurances.

Further bridge-building was contributed by Wendell Willkie, defeated Republican candidate for the presidency in 1940. Making a goodwill trip to Moscow in August 1942, he called for a speedy second front, and raised eyebrows by adding that American military leaders "will need some public prodding."

In his book, *One World*, Willkie observed that the average Russian "naturally finds some good in a system that has improved his own lot, and has a tendency to forget the ruthless means by which it has been brought about. This may be difficult for an American to believe or like. . . . Russia is an effective society. It works."

By now Stalin was highly popular with American correspondents, who referred to him fondly as "Uncle Joe." His new wartime image did much to soften memories of the Moscow trials, the invasion of Finland, and the Nazi-Soviet pact.

At the same time Stalin sought to erase the image many Russians had been given of the Americans and British as greedy capitalist societies. "In England and the United States there are elementary democratic freedoms," he now conceded, "and there exist professional labor and employees' unions, labor parties, and parliaments."

Stalin displayed a knowledge of American military history. Ordering the Red Army to make strategic retreats when necessary to avoid encirclement, he explained to an American general that Marshal Semën Timoshenko was his "George Washington," because Washington had saved the American Revolution by retreating from Philadelphia. Stalin called Marshal Georgi Zhukov "my George B. McClellan. . . . Like McClellan he always wants more men, more cannon, more guns, more planes. But—unlike McClellan—Zhukov has never lost a battle!"

As the year wore on, it became clear that no second front could be opened in Europe in 1942. Churchill flew to Moscow to inform Stalin, who was upset and freshly suspicious.

Why had FDR misled him? Was there a secret Anglo-American plan to bleed the Soviet Union as much as possible, simultaneously weakening the Nazi forces, before the Allies committed armies to a second front?

When the Russians won the battle of Stalingrad in January 1943, FDR congratulated Stalin on the Red Army's "magnificent achievements unsurpassed in all history." He declared, "The Red Army and the Russian people have surely started the Hitler forces on the road to ultimate defeat and have earned the lasting admiration of the people of the United States."

Stalin was disappointed in May 1943 when, instead of the second front he had been promised, the Allies invaded North Africa to engage Rommel's forces in the Middle East. The invasion would have little effect on forcing Hitler to divert Nazi divisions fighting on the Russian front. But it could, by securing the Mediterranean, shorten by thousands of miles the shipping lanes over which war supplies were flowing from the United States to the Soviet Union.

Making the best of it, Stalin sent congratulations to FDR for "the brilliant victory which has resulted in the liberation of Bizerte and Tunis from Hitler tyranny." When he learned that the Allies were not going to be able to open a second front until the spring of 1944, however, he grew bitter.

"Your decision," he wrote FDR, "creates exceptional difficulties for the Soviet Union, which, straining all its resources, for the past two years has been engaged against the main forces of Germany and its satellites, and leaves the Soviet Army, which is fighting not only for its country, but also for its Allies, to do the job alone, almost single-handed."

Stalin's resentment increased when Mussolini was overthrown, and the Allies occupied Italy without inviting participation by the USSR. Stalin complained to FDR, "I have to tell you that it is impossible to tolerate the situation any longer."

Until now he had evaded a face-to-face meeting with the president, explaining that pressing war duties confined him to Russia. But now he agreed to meet FDR and Churchill in Teheran, Iran, to iron out their differences.

When Roosevelt arrived in late November 1943, Stalin persuaded him to stay at Iran's Soviet embassy because Russian Intelligence had learned of a Nazi plot against FDR's life. The British were annoyed, believing that Stalin was maneuvering to get FDR on his side against Churchill.

Nikita Khrushchev, who was at Teheran with Stalin,

observed, "Stalin often found Roosevelt siding with him against Churchill, thus, Stalin's personal sympathies were definitely reserved for Roosevelt."

Churchill and Stalin clashed on where the second front ought to be opened. Churchill wanted to land troops in the south of Europe, primarily to keep postwar control of Greece and Yugoslavia in British hands. FDR supported Stalin's insistence that the Western invasion must take place in northern France, to crush the Nazi forces in a vise between the two Allied armies. Stalin promised, in turn, that Russia would enter the Japanese war within six months after Hitler's defeat, and would cooperate in organizing the UN.

Returning from Teheran, FDR told his son Elliott that he considered his principal achievement there convincing Stalin "that the United States and Great Britain were not allied in one common bloc against the Soviet Union. . . . The one thing that would upset the applecart, after the war, is if the world is divided again, Russia against England and us. That's our big job now, and that'll be our big job tomorrow, too."

FDR viewed Stalin as "a man hewn out of granite," but was impressed with his quick grasp of problems and his wit. "I believe Stalin is truly representative of the heart and soul of Russia," he declared, "and I believe that we are going to get along very well with him and the Russian people—very well indeed." He wrote Stalin that he considered Teheran "assurance not only of our ability to wage war together, but also to work for the peace to come in utmost harmony."

Replying, Stalin echoed his sentiments and dropped a hint that it would best be proved by a swift opening of the second front: "I hope the common enemy of our peoples—Hitler Germany—will soon come to feel this."

As preparations for the second front were under way in

May 1944, Russian confidence in American motives was shaken by a swaggering, widely reported speech made in England by U.S. Gen. George Patton. Patton boasted that it was the "destiny" of the United States and Britain to "rule the world" after the war. Appalled, Gen. Dwight D. Eisenhower, commander of the Allied forces in the West, strongly disavowed the speech. But the damage had been done.

Relations between Soviet officialdom and Americans in the USSR grew more formal. Correspondent Ella Winter wrote, "Everywhere one felt hampered. I could not see my old acquaintances of 1931 in their homes; they would receive me only in the company of officials."

The opening of the Second Front on June 6, 1944, abruptly restored Americans to favor in Moscow. American embassy press attaché Frederick Barghoorn reported, "Americans in Moscow during the summer of 1944 were lionized by their Soviet friends. . . . I visited several high officials of the Ministry of Education . . . who assured me that Russians since June 6 had taken a 'very special interest' in America and that study of the English language was growing by leaps and bounds."

Stalin called the Normandy invasion "an achievement of the highest order." Soon afterward, however, he could not resist pointing out that its success had been made possible only because the Red Army was pinning down the main Nazi forces.

In the new euphoria created by the Second Front, Mikoyan invited Eric Johnston, president of the U.S. Chamber of Commerce, to tour Soviet war production facilities in the Urals, Siberia, and Central Asia, as a prelude to postwar trade discussions. American correspondents were allowed to accompany him.

At a banquet given Johnston in Moscow, Johnston told

Soviet trade officials, "We in America have a proverb which says that your only true friend is the one who knows the worst about you and still likes you." Soviet-American differences in economic systems, he declared, need not be a barrier to good relations after the war. His speech, applauded as also reflecting Soviet policy, was given wide circulation.

Gratified by the Second Front, which foreshadowed the certain defeat of the Nazis, Russians manifested a new surge of affection for the Americans, stopping them on the street and in parks to congratulate them. Soviet intellectuals, teachers, engineers, doctors, and specialists of all kinds eagerly sought contacts with their American counterparts.

Lectures by Soviet fliers, artists, and journalists returning from the United States were packed to the doors. Soviet teachers, unable to answer a flood of questions by curious students, asked for more literature about the United States. Moscow's State Institute of the Soviet Encyclopedia responded by publishing an informative handbook, *The United States of America*, the first collection of facts about American history, geography, industry, agriculture, education, politics, health, art, science, and defense to be published in the Soviet Union.

In January 1945 a desperate Nazi counterattack against the Anglo-American forces in France, the Battle of the Bulge, brought about an appeal from Eisenhower for a quick new Soviet offensive. Stalin responded by launching one ahead of schedule, despite unfavorable weather conditions. The Nazis were forced to withdraw armored units from the Ardennes and rush them to the eastern front. Still unable to stop the Red Army, they were driven back through Poland, East Prussia, and Silesia to less than fifty miles from Berlin.

"They will have to disperse their reserves between the two fronts," Stalin wrote FDR, "and . . . relinquish the offensive on the Western Front. I am glad that this circumstance will ease the position of the Allied troops in the West and expedite . . . the offensive planned by General Eisenhower."

American troops were filled with admiration for the fighting prowess of the Russians. At one prisoner-of-war camp near Vienna, American prisoners organized a group to collect food for Soviet POWs at another camp nearby.

"Many of us were receiving Red Cross packages, and we collected canned meat, chocolate, and cigarettes for the Russians," recalled former B-17 machine gunner Frank Batterson. "We knew they were starving. First we tried to throw food over the barbed wire to them during our walks, but the guards got most of it. Then we said we wouldn't eat until the Germans handed the food over to the Russians, and that did it."

Eisenhower sent staff members to Moscow to arrange closer coordination between the Russian and American forces, to make sure that as they ground the Nazi armies between them they would not unknowingly hurt each other. For this reason he decided to stop the Allied advance on the line of the Elbe River, letting the Russians take Berlin.

In any event, Eisenhower's armies were still over three hundred miles from Berlin when Marshal Georgi Zhukov began his final assault on the enemy capital. Churchill wanted to race the Red Army to Berlin, but Eisenhower saw no military sense in it. U.S. Chief of Staff George C. Marshall agreed, telling Eisenhower, "I would be loath to hazard American lives for purely political purposes." Stopping at the Elbe would prevent an estimated 100,000 U.S. casualties.

With the downfall of Hitler imminent, Stalin, Roosevelt, and Churchill arranged to meet at the Soviet Black Sea port of Yalta, to draw final military plans for the defeat of Germany and Japan, and to settle the political future of postwar Europe. At Yalta Harry Hopkins prepared a position paper as a guide for the American delegation.

"We know that we and Russia are the two most powerful nations in the world in manpower and raw materials," he wrote. "We know that we have been able to fight side by side with the Russians in the greatest war in all history. . . . Russia's interests . . . do not afford an opportunity for a major difference with us in foreign affairs. We believe we are mutually dependent upon each other for economic reasons."

Stalin, however, would not consent to participate in the proposed United Nations until it was agreed that each major power would have an absolute right of veto in the Security Council. He reminded his allies that the League of Nations had expelled the Soviet Union during the Russo-Finnish War—"the same League that never lifted a finger to stop Hitler or any single act of aggression!"

Stalin won his demand that territory be stripped from Germany in the west to repay Poland for land the USSR had annexed in the east. But he and Churchill clashed over the question of a postwar government for Poland. Churchill insisted that the London-based Polish government-in-exile must be restored to power. Stalin indicated that he meant to call the tune in the Soviet Union's east European backyard, through which it had been invaded.

"It is not only a question of honor for Russia," he told his allies, "but one of life and death. . . . Throughout history Poland has been the corridor for attack on Russia."

The issue was something of a sore point between FDR, who wanted free elections to let the Polish people choose their own government, and Stalin, who insisted that Russian security required a friendly government in Warsaw.

"Words have a different connotation to the Soviets than they have to us," Ambassador W. Averell Harriman observed to Roosevelt. "When they speak of insisting on 'friendly governments' in their neighboring countries, they have in mind something quite different from what we would mean."

Big Three recognition for the Soviet-sponsored Polish government of occupation was finally agreed upon when Stalin promised to reorganize it on a broader basis.

Stalin struck a secret bargain at Yalta with Roosevelt, promising to enter the war against Japan as soon as Germany was defeated, in exchange for Port Arthur, Dairen, the Kuril Islands, and control of the Eastern Chinese Railway. "I only want to have returned to Russia what the Japanese have taken from my country," Stalin said, referring to the 1904 war.

"That seems a reasonable suggestion," FDR nodded.

Stalin reached an understanding with his allies that the Western powers' sphere of influence would include Greece, Yugoslavia, and Italy, while the USSR would exercise authority in eastern Europe. "Each side," observed historian Henry Steele Commager, "made concessions not only to the other but to reality." FDR also hoped that a generous attitude toward Stalin would make him a cooperative postwar partner.

Stalin grew suspicious, however, when Germans trapped in Italy were permitted to surrender to the Western Allies, and other Nazi units in Germany sought to escape Russian capture by offering to surrender to the Americans. Soviet Intelligence reported rumors that the Western Allies were considering a separate peace with the Germans, leaving

Nazi forces in the east free to continue fighting and weakening the Red Army.

Stalin relayed his suspicions bluntly to FDR.

Indignant, the American president replied, "It would be one of the great tragedies of history if at the very moment of the victory now within our grasp, such distrust, such lack of faith should prejudice the entire undertaking after the colossal losses of life, materiel, and treasure involved. Frankly I cannot avoid a feeling of bitter resentment toward your informers, whoever they are, for such vile misrepresentations of my actions or of those of my subordinates."

But Stalin was not reassured. He was determined, come what may, to hang onto full control of eastern Europe as a vast buffer area to make another invasion of Russia impossible. Supporting an all-Communist regime in Poland, he also failed to send Molotov to the San Francisco Conference for the opening session of the United Nations when it became apparent that demands would be raised for self-determination by the Poles.

Roosevelt was shocked. A dying man, the president was nevertheless unwilling to relinquish his dream of a peaceful postwar world. On his last day of life, he wrote to Churchill urging him to "minimize the general Soviet problem as much as possible because these problems, in one form or another, seem to arise every day, and most of them straighten out."

Roosevelt died on April 12, 1945, as American army units crossed the Elbe River and were ordered by Eisenhower to wait there for the linkup with Russian troops.

News of FDR's death reached Moscow close to midnight. Harriman immediately went to see Stalin and told him. Clearly moved by the news, Stalin was also worried about its implications. He knew Roosevelt; he did not know the new president, Harry S. Truman.

Harriman suggested to Stalin that the best way he could demonstrate Russian respect for Roosevelt was to honor the late president's urgent wish for Soviet participation in the United Nations. Stalin agreed to send Molotov to San Francisco, and gave him instructions to stop off in Washington to see Truman.

Stalin had to know what kind of an American president he would be dealing with in the postwar world.

Visiting the White House on April 22, 1945, Molotov was stunned when Truman subjected him to an angry tirade because Stalin wasn't carrying out his Yalta promise to include British-backed Polish exiles in the Warsaw government. Truman ignored the fact that Britain was also denying free elections to the people of Greece, Iraq, Egypt, and Jordan, and that Poland, as well as all East European countries except Czechoslovakia, had always been dictatorships.

"I made up my mind that I would lay it on the line with Molotov," Truman later revealed. Convinced "the Russians needed us more than we needed them," he warned Molotov that if there were any further breaches of the Yalta agreement, the United States would no longer consider it binding, and the UN would be organized with or without the USSR.

That sounded to Molotov like a threat to use the UN as a means of policing the Soviet Union.

"I have never been talked to in my life like this!" he protested indignantly. Truman snapped, "Carry out your agreements and you won't get talked to like this."

Three days later Truman received an angry message from Stalin pointing out that Poland was a border problem for the Soviet Union, but not for the United States or England.

"You, apparently, do not agree that the Soviet Union has a right to make efforts that there should exist in Poland a government friendly toward the Soviet Union . . . [not] hostile toward it," Stalin wrote. But had Truman or Churchill consulted him about the new governments established in Greece and Belgium? And had Stalin sought to interfere in spheres he recognized as necessary for Britain's security?

"I am ready to fulfill your request and do everything possible to reach a harmonious solution," he declared. "But you demand too much . . . that I renounce the interests of security of the Soviet Union. . . . I cannot turn against my country."

Even as the air grew chillier on the diplomatic peaks, a joyful linkup took place on April 23, 1945, on the battlefields between the American armies and advance elements of the Red Army reaching the west bank of the Elbe.

"Our men sighted troop movements ahead," recalled Soviet physicist Ivan Samchuk, who reached the Elbe that day at the head of a Soviet rifle corps. "What if they were Germans? We dug in and waited. There were shouts of 'Who goes there?' in Russian, but no reply. We decided to fire a few shots in the air. Suddenly several soldiers emerged from their shelter and, waving their trench caps, shouted: 'America! Stalingrad!' It was a historic moment. News of the Americans' approach spread like lightning to our armies. General rejoicing began."

There were wild whoops of delight, hand-pumping, hugging, vodka-drinking, rations-sharing, spontaneous demonstrations of mutual admiration, exchanges of medals, buttons, and insignia. "The language barrier was no barrier at all," Samchuk related. "We talked to one another with gestures and single words."

American correspondent Martha Gellhorn noted Soviet women soldiers with the Red Army: "These women were uniformed like the men, and equally armed, and were young . . . tough as prizefighters. We were told that the women were wonderful snipers and that they served as MPs. . . . They looked as if no hardship would be too much for them, no roads too long, no winter too cruel, no danger too great."

Women soldiers presented flowers to the GIs. Exuberant Russian-American dances were held to celebrate the occasion.

Gen. Omar Bradley made the tribute more formal in his order of the day: "American troops of the Twelfth Army Group joined forces with Soviet elements of Marshal Konev's First Ukrainian Army Group. These armies have come down from the ruins of Stalingrad and Sevastopol, across the scorched cities of the Ukraine. In two years they have smashed fourteen hundred miles through the German Army to drive the enemy from Russia and pursue him to the Elbe."

Presenting Ivan Samchuk with the Legion of Merit, U.S. Gen. Ernest Harmon expressed the hopes of the tired Russian and American soldiers at the Elbe: "People who have experienced the adversities of war will not find it hard to settle the question of peace. We must do everything possible to keep war from happening again."

The meeting at the Elbe remained an inspirational symbol down through the years. On its tenth anniversary, Russian veterans invited their former American comrades-in-arms to Moscow for a deeply emotional reunion. Subsequent reunions were held in both Moscow and Washington.

Unconcerned with the diplomatic quarrel between Truman and Stalin, Eisenhower retained only the warmest feelings toward the Russians. He refused to have anything to do with the frantic attempts of the Nazis to escape retribution at the hands of the Red Army. Churchill phoned to report, "Ike, we have an official offer from Himmler to surrender to us, but not to Russia." Eisenhower replied, "Wrap it up in diplomatic language, and tell him to go to hell." He insisted upon unconditional German surrender—to *all* the Allies.

The Nazis had good reason to wish themselves in American or British hands. They had killed 405,000 Americans and 375,000 British, but 20 million Russians —half of these civilians and prisoners of war murdered or tortured to death by Nazi troops on Russian soil.

On May 7, 1945, with Hitler a suicide in his Berlin bunker, the Germans were forced to surrender unconditionally.

There were tremendous celebrations in the United States and in the Soviet Union. In a great surge of emotion, many American liberals joined the American Communist party, including such well-known authors as Theodore Dreiser.

Germany was divided into East and West zones of occupation. Berlin, encircled by East Germany, was likewise divided. Eisenhower promptly struck up a warm friendship with his opposite number, Soviet Marshal Georgi Zhukov.

A reporter asked the American commander if he felt that he would have any trouble cooperating with the Russians.

"On my level, none," Eisenhower replied. "I have found the individual Russian one of the friendliest persons in the world. He likes to talk with us, laugh with us. . . . [He bears] a marked similarity to what we call the average American."

He and Zhukov encouraged the exchange of social visits between Russians and Americans. "These affairs seemed to be thoroughly enjoyed by both sides," Eisenhower related. "The Russians love entertainment and genuinely appreciate any kind of music; so the jokes, companionship, and the orchestras at a dinner made all these occasions successful."

When he and Zhukov had problems about their respective German zones, Eisenhower made a point of rendering prompt decisions without checking first with Washington. "If I sent such small details to Washington for decision I would be fired," he explained to the impressed Zhukov, who began demanding and getting the same authority from Moscow.

Eisenhower helped enhance his Russian friend's power to negotiate independently during a visit to Moscow. He told Stalin, "Of course Marshal Zhukov and I get along splendidly. This is because great and powerful countries like yours and mine can afford to give their proconsuls in the field a sufficient amount of authority to achieve accord. . . . [With] such great leeway in reaching agreement, we two usually overcome the little obstacles we encounter."

"There is no sense in sending a delegate somewhere if he is merely to be an errand boy," Stalin agreed.

Later, in gratitude, Zhukov unbuckled an exquisite gold and ivory dagger from his belt and presented it to his American friend as a token of affectionate regard.

Back in Washington, Eisenhower's fondness for the Russians was not shared by many military officers and bureaucrats, whose old hostility toward the Soviet Union began to reemerge once the crisis in Europe was over.

One of the first acts of the Truman administration was to terminate, without warning, all Lend-Lease aid to the

Soviet Union. This was done despite Russia's staggering war losses—32,000 factories, 15 large cities, 1,710 towns, 6 million buildings, 90,000 bridges, 70,000 villages destroyed. The Germans had also carried off 200 million cows and chickens, and had wrecked 1,135 coal mines, 3,000 oil wells, and 10,000 power stations. And 25 million Russians were homeless.

When the Soviet government requested a $6 billion postwar loan to put the country back on its feet, the State Department "lost" the request, then turned it down. The Russians were left with no alternative but to seize the assets of satellite nations in eastern Europe that they had taken from the Nazis, in order to achieve recovery and feed their own people.

President Truman later admitted that it had been wrong to cut off Lend-Lease abruptly: "It should have been done on a gradual basis which would not have made it appear as if somebody had been deliberately snubbed. After all, we had extracted an agreement from the Russians at Yalta that they would be in the Japanese war three months after the Germans folded up. There was, at this time, a friendly feeling in America toward Russia because the Russians, though fighting for their own survival, had saved us many lives in the war."

Truman sent Harry Hopkins to Moscow to placate Stalin. Stalin told Hopkins angrily that the abrupt termination of Lend-Lease had been "unfortunate and even brutal," adding that if it was "designed as pressure on the Russians in order to soften them up, then it was a fundamental mistake."

Hopkins convinced him that both the cutoff and the misplacement of Russia's loan request had been bureaucratic errors, and did not reflect Truman administration policy. Mollified, Stalin agreed to meet with

Truman and Churchill at Potsdam, Germany, to discuss postwar problems and cooperation.

Truman came to Potsdam in late July 1945 determined to contain Communist influence. At a personal level he found that he liked Stalin, who spoke "straight from the shoulder." But because of the inauspicious beginning of their relationship, Stalin distrusted Truman, who also lacked Roosevelt's easy charm and diplomatic skill.

As Khrushchev viewed Truman at Potsdam, "he had neither an ounce of statesmanship nor a flexible mind," and "was hostile and spiteful toward the Soviet Union. I can't imagine how anyone ever considered Truman worthy of the vice-presidency, much less the presidency."

Truman insisted on elections in Poland and in East European countries which had never had them, and which had strong Fascist movements. Stalin flatly refused. Secretary of War Henry L. Stimson pointed out to Truman that outside of the United States and Britain, few countries understood or cared for free elections, adding that "the Russians perhaps were more realistic than we were in regard to their own security."

Stalin revealed to Truman that Tokyo had been making peace overtures through the Kremlin, but repeated Russia's pledge to enter the Pacific war on August 8. Truman, meanwhile, received word that the first test of the American atom bomb had been successful. Feeling that he should inform Stalin, he mentioned casually that the United States now had "a new weapon of unusual destructive force."

"I'm glad to hear it," Stalin replied mildly, "and hope we will make good use of it against the Japanese." He displayed no surprise or special interest; his Intelligence network had already told him about the Americans' A-bomb.

A few days after the Potsdam Conference, Stalin invited

Eisenhower to visit the Soviet Union as a guest of the Red Army, with Zhukov as his host. Flying to Moscow, Eisenhower was appalled at not seeing a house standing between the western Soviet border and the area around Moscow.

"Almost everything had been destroyed," he observed. ". . . All this would have embittered any people; it would have been completely astonishing if the Russians had not had a more direct and personal vindictiveness toward the Germans . . . [than] countries far removed from the scene of hostilities."

Stalin invited Eisenhower and Ambassador Harriman to join him on top of Lenin's tomb, where no foreigner had ever set foot before, to review a huge sports parade in Red Square.

"We stood for five hours on the tomb while the show went on," Eisenhower related. "None of us had ever witnessed anything remotely similar. . . . Every kind of folk dance, mass exercise, acrobatic feat, and athletic exhibition was executed with flawless precision."

After a dinner in his honor, films were screened of Zhukov's capture of Berlin. By way of compliment, Eisenhower joked to his interpreter, "Tell Marshal Zhukov that if he ever loses his job in the Soviet Union he can, on the evidence of this picture, surely get one in Hollywood." Stalin, taking him seriously, assured Eisenhower, "Marshal Zhukov will never be without a job in the Soviet Union."

Expressing views he knew would reach Truman, Stalin told Eisenhower, "We must get your technicians to help us in our engineering and construction problems, and we want to know more about mass production methods in factories. We know we are behind in these things and we know that you can help us."

In a tour of the Soviet Union, Eisenhower was shown

anything he wanted to see. At a Leningrad luncheon in his honor, his son John was called upon to propose a toast.

"To the common soldier of the great Red Army!"

Zhukov was delighted. "It takes a young lieutenant to remind us old generals," he told John Eisenhower's father, "who *really* won the war."

On August 9 the Red Army in Siberia launched a furiously rolling attack with tanks, infantry, and artillery across the Manchurian border, sending Japanese troops reeling back.

Russia's attack, later observed Gen. Claire Chennault, commander of the U.S. Air Force in China, forced Tokyo to surrender, and would have done so "even if no atomic bomb had been dropped." The chief reason the bomb was dropped on Hiroshima and Nagasaki, according to physicist Leo Szilard, was because Secretary of State James Byrnes wanted Truman to impress Stalin with American nuclear power, "to make Russia more manageable in Europe." The War Department also wanted to force Japan's surrender quickly before the Soviet Union could claim a full share of the victory in the Pacific.

On August 14, 1945, Japan surrendered, ending the Second World War. Differences between the United States and the Soviet Union grew rapidly over the nature of the peace.

Secretary of War Stimson argued within Truman's cabinet that it was inconsistent for the United States "to hang on to the exaggerated views of the Monroe Doctrine [for Latin America] and at the same time butt into every question that comes up in Central Europe." Acceptance of Soviet and American spheres of influence, Stimson insisted, was the only logical way to avoid a "head-on collision with the USSR."

He joined Secretary of Commerce Henry Wallace in urging that American nuclear knowledge should be shared with the Soviet Union for the peaceful development of energy.

Eisenhower and Zhukov continued to cooperate with one another. On November 7 Zhukov told his American counterpart, "If the United States and Russia will only stand together through thick and thin, success is certain for the United Nations. If we are partners, there are no other countries . . . that would dare go to war when we forbade it."

Despite the forces working to unite Moscow and Washington in the postwar world, Truman was convinced by his advisers that Stalin was bent on spreading Communist revolution. But as historian Arthur Schlesinger points out, Stalin was all too ready to accept a policy of live and let live: "His initial objectives were very probably not world conquest but Russian security." Far from stimulating revolution, the Russians sought to dampen it in China, France, Italy, and Greece.

Needing American postwar aid, Stalin tried to reassure Washington by acting as a stabilizing force in Europe. He even told Milovan Djilas of Yugoslavia, "The uprising in Greece must be stopped, and as quickly as possible."

By December 1945, however, Truman had made up his mind to impose on the Soviet Union his view of how the postwar world should be organized. He authorized Secretary of State Byrnes to adopt a "get tough" policy toward Stalin.

The cold war had begun.

PART IV

★ ☆

THE COLD WAR
1946-1971

"The dropping of the atomic bomb," observed British physicist P. M. S. Blackett, "was not so much the last military act of the Second World War, as the first major operation of the cold diplomatic war with Russia."

Correspondent Alexander Werth described the reaction to Hiroshima in Moscow: "In the press there was only a brief summary of President Truman's first statement. . . . I asked the editor of one important paper why, and he said; 'Because our people are much too upset by the whole damned thing.' And another Russian said to me in a tone of genuine melancholy: 'Our people really thought that this war would be our last war with the Capitalist world; but now we wonder.' "

Russian suspicions were not lulled when Truman proposed Bernard Baruch's plan to share atomic knowledge if Moscow agreed to give up trying to make its own A-bomb. The Kremlin rejected this offer as a scheme to force military inferiority on the USSR, with the American air force controlling the skies, the American navy controlling the seas, and American bases encircling the Soviet Union.

Washington pointed out that most American ground

forces had been demobilized, while large Russian forces were being kept in East Europe. But much of the Red Army was unmechanized. The USSR itself was exhausted physically and psychologically, the country in ruins, much of its manpower dead.

Stalin asked Truman and Churchill to agree upon reparations from German industry for war damage to the Soviet Union's devastated factories, power plants, machinery, railway equipment, homes, schools, and hospitals. Truman not only refused but demanded over a billion dollars for Lend-Lease supplies he charged the Russians had not used in the war.

Washington also protested Soviet hegemony over East Europe. In the American view, Stalin had no right to impose Communist forms of government upon East Europeans.

From Moscow's point of view, Truman was violating Roosevelt's understanding with Stalin at Yalta. The USSR had made it clear that it would never again allow East Europe to be used as an invasion corridor. And since German reparations were being denied the Russians to rebuild their shattered economy, East European nations, which had supplied troops to Hitler's invasion forces, would have to contribute their share.

Washington viewed Moscow's consolidation of East Europe as a threat to West Europe. Moscow saw the Truman Doctrine, the Marshall Plan, and NATO as steps toward reimposing capitalist encirclement of the Soviet Union to destroy it.

In the UN Russians proposed banning all atomic weapons, destroying stockpiles, prohibiting war propaganda, and reducing all armaments and armed forces by one-third.

The Truman administration rejected the Soviet proposal

as insincere propaganda. An increasingly conservative Congress, convinced that the Soviet Union could never produce an atom bomb of its own, insisted that the United States should keep its "secret" until the Russians agreed to American terms. They should also be denied loans and trade until they submitted to American political demands for East Europe and Germany.

Henry Wallace, now secretary of commerce, warned that it was an illusion to imagine that Soviet scientists could not produce their own nuclear weapons. In a letter to Truman he urged discussing "with the Russians in a friendly way their long range economic problems. . . . Much of the recent Soviet behavior which has caused us concern has been the result of their dire economic needs and of their disturbed sense of security . . . fears of 'capitalist encirclement.' " Wallace urged "proving to them that we want to trade with them and to cement our economic relations with them."

"I ignored this letter of Wallace's," Truman said.

On February 28, 1946, Secretary of State James Byrnes hinted in a speech the beginning of a new "firm" policy toward the Soviet Union. Truman shocked Wallace five days later by appearing with Winston Churchill, who had been voted out of office by the British Labour party, when Churchill made his famous "iron curtain" speech at Fulton, Missouri. Churchill accused Stalin of having enslaved the countries of East Europe behind an iron curtain of communism, and warned that only military strength could prevent West Europe's annexation.

Wallace immediately protested to Truman, "Getting tough never bought anything real and lasting—whether for schoolyard bullies or world powers. The tougher we get, the tougher the Russians will get." But Truman had already accepted a new foreign policy shaped by the Pentagon, which considered it the responsibility of the United States, as world leader, to act as an international policeman and check revolutions everywhere. The Soviet Union was alleged to be behind all local revolutionary movements. If revolutions abroad were not crushed, eventually Americans would presumably have to fight communism on the shores of California and the eastern seaboard.

On May Day Stalin told the Red Army, "We should not forget for a single minute the intrigues of international reaction, which is hatching plans for a new war."

Wallace persisted in trying to turn Truman from the hard line he had taken toward the Russians. In July he wrote the president pointing out that four-fifths of the American budget was being spent on war-related purposes, and that the Russians had reason to fear a surprise attack. "How would it look to us," he asked, "if Russia had the 10,000-mile bombers and air bases within a thousand miles of our coastlines, and we did not?" He urged Truman to take steps to offer "reasonable Russian guarantees of security."

Instead, when Truman sent Byrnes to Paris to negotiate the postwar peace treaty with the Russians, he instructed the secretary of state to take a tough stance. Wallace threw a bombshell into these negotiations by a speech in New York's Madison Square Garden.

"We have no more business in the *political* affairs of eastern Europe," he insisted, "than Russia has in the *political* affairs of Latin America, western Europe, and the United States. . . . Whether we like it or not, the Russians will try to socialize their sphere of influence, just as we try to democratize our sphere of influence."

Byrnes sent a furious teletype to Truman demanding that Wallace be forced to resign. Truman promptly obliged.

★ ☆

All through 1946 Greek guerrillas fought to overthrow a British-supported monarchy which, according to the London *Times*, beat and tortured political opponents seized in mass arrests. By February 1947 London told the Truman administration that it could no longer afford to prop up the reactionary regimes in Greece and Turkey. Truman decided to take over this task to secure them as anti-Soviet air and naval bases.

"We did not have to decide," Byrnes explained, "that the Turkish government and Greek monarchy were outstanding examples of free and democratic governments."

Truman assumed that Stalin was aiding and abetting, if not actually directing, a Communist revolution in Greece. In actual fact, Stalin opposed Greek revolution, just as he did revolution in China, where he supported Chiang Kai-shek. Unlike Trotsky, Stalin was far less interested in world revolution than in a stable world peace which would permit the war-prostrated Soviet economy to recover and rebuild.

Truman asked Congress for a huge military and economic aid program for Greece and Turkey, declaring it essential to save them from communism. Gen. George Marshall, succeeding Byrnes as secretary of state, thought Truman had exaggerated the situation. Truman admitted it, explaining it was the only way he could alarm Congress into voting the funds.

Wallace accused Truman of betraying "the great tradition of America" by plunging the nation into a "reckless adventure" that would usher in a "century of fear."

But George F. Kennan, the State Department's expert on the USSR, advised Truman and Marshall, "The United States cannot expect in the foreseeable future to enjoy political intimacy with the Soviet regime. It must continue to regard the Soviet Union as a rival, not a partner, in the political arena." Architect of the Truman administration's cold war policy of "containment," Kennan urged building U.S. military strength to meet Soviet pressure wherever it developed.

Marshall, apprehensive that shaky postwar governments in western Europe would collapse and become prey to revolution, prepared a program of economic aid to help them survive. The Russians denounced the Marshall Plan as an attempt to keep reactionary governments in place. Moscow replied by reviving the Comintern, dissolved during World War II, as the Cominform. Opposing U.S. "expansion and aggression," it coordinated the work of Communist parties in nine European countries.

In March 1948 the U.S. Department of Commerce applied discriminatory regulations to reduce exports to the USSR.

Outraged by Truman's anti-Soviet policies, Wallace broke away from the Democratic party to oppose his reelection as the candidate of the new Progressive party. But the old FDR New Deal leaders who backed Wallace were unable to persuade more than 1,100,000 Americans, and Truman was reelected over Dewey by a narrow margin. Part of the reason had to do with a show of American support for the president's position during the Soviet blockade of Berlin.

Each of the four World War II allies occupied a zone within the city, which was entirely surrounded by Russian-occupied East Germany. In June 1948 a dispute over currency led the Russians to apply pressure by sealing off all highway, rail, and river traffic between Berlin and West Germany.

"Technical difficulties," said Soviet authorities.

"Our position in Berlin was precarious," Truman noted. "If we wished to remain there, we would have to make a show of strength. But there was always the risk that Russian reaction might lead to war." His solution was to introduce an airlift of supplies from West Germany into Berlin. Lasting 321 days, it brought in over forty-five hundred tons of supplies daily to over two million West Berliners. The Russians finally agreed to call off the blockade and negotiate East-West differences.

As the cold war burgeoned, anti-Communist hysteria whipped up by political demagogues made it dangerous for Americans known to favor friendly relations with the Soviet Union.

In the Soviet Union, Marshal Zhukov was relegated to obscurity because of his wartime friendship with Eisenhower.

In May 1949 Truman sent Dean Acheson, his new secretary of state, to Paris for a foreign ministers' conference. Acheson demanded that the Russians agree to reunify East and West Germany, and reduce their standing army in East Europe.

"He is so *totally* anti-Soviet and is going to be so *completely* tough," Sen. Arthur Vandenberg, Republican leader for foreign affairs, wrote his wife, "that I really doubt whether there is any chance at all for a Paris agreement."

When this prophecy proved correct, Acheson organized the North Atlantic Treaty Alliance, signed by a dozen nations. Under NATO's defense pact, the United States agreed to rearm them and shield them with its nuclear bombing power.

George F. Kennan admitted eight years later that the State Department had not considered a Soviet attack on western Europe a serious possibility. What had really concerned both Marshall and Acheson, Kennan revealed, was "the Communist danger in its most threatening form —as an *internal* problem, that is of Western society." Marshall had warned he would cut off aid funds to any country which *voted* itself Communist.

NATO, in short, was primarily a political, not military, maneuver against the Soviet Union. Countries receiving NATO funds, moreover, were permitted to use them to contain *non*-Communist revolutions in Algeria, Indochina, and the Portuguese colonies in Africa.

The Russian response to NATO came in September 1949 with the explosion of its own atomic bomb, three years sooner than American experts had believed possible. The U.S. monopoly on nuclear weapons had been broken, altering not only the balance of power but the kind of world we all live in.

Shocked, Truman spurred American scientists to speed the development of a superweapon—the H-bomb. Both nations became locked into a deadly and expensive arms race.

The end of World War II had left Korea divided in half—a Soviet-supported Communist regime in the north, an American-supported capitalist regime in the south. On June 24, 1950, North Korean troops suddenly invaded South Korea across the 38th parallel boundary. Truman at once ordered U.S. air and naval forces to the aid of the Seoul regime. The UN authorized a "police action" against North Korea, utilizing chiefly American forces under MacArthur as UN commander.

The cold war heated up. Under Allan Dulles, the CIA stepped up its anti-Soviet campaign. Radio Free Europe began broadcasting anti-Communist propaganda to East

European countries. Secretly funded by the CIA to subvert their Communist regimes, it masqueraded as a private organization to which Americans were urged to contribute. Radio Liberty also beamed anti-Soviet propaganda directly at the USSR in Russian. Half a billion dollars were spent on both projects.

Years later chairman William Fulbright of the Senate Foreign Relations Committee accused the White House of having deceived both Americans and East Europeans about the fact that these "private" stations were secret CIA projects.

In July 1951 Congress abrogated the Soviet-American trade agreement of 1937. In November, with the fighting still raging in Korea, Senate majority leader Lyndon B. Johnson issued a bitter warning to the Soviet Union.

"The next aggression will be the last," he threatened. ". . . We will strike back, not just at your satellites, but at you . . . with all the dreaded might that is within our control, and it will be a crushing blow."

But George Kennan, who had blueprinted the cold war, now considered it a blunder. "We will get nowhere with an attitude of emotional indignation directed toward an entire people," he advised Truman.

Eisenhower, appointed to head NATO in 1951, also pleaded for common sense. He suggested, "We must learn in this world to accommodate ourselves so that we may live at peace with others whose basic philosophy may be very different."

Prime Minister Jawaharlal Nehru of India told U.S. Ambassador Chester Bowles that American foreign policy was based on a number of assumptions he considered "dangerously wrong." He chided the American belief that the United States was a target of a "world-wide Communist conspiracy." The Soviet Union and Red China were bitter enemies, Nehru pointed out to Bowles, far more in conflict with each other than with Washington. And the U.S. was wrong in misjudging revolutions in various parts of the world as the work of Peking and Moscow; they were actually nationalistic movements for freedom and independence.

In March 1952 Moscow accused the United States of waging germ warfare against the North Koreans. In May the State Department banned travel by American citizens to the Soviet Union or any Communist country in East Europe.

The 1952 presidential campaign pitted Republican candidate Dwight Eisenhower against Adlai Stevenson for the Democrats.

Despite the Korean War, Stevenson called for coexistence and friendly competition with the Soviet Union. Eisenhower's similar views were curbed by his rigidly anti-Communist foreign policy adviser, John Foster Dulles, who became secretary of state after Eisenhower's sweeping victory.

Dulles promptly broadcast a promise to the people of East Europe that they could count on the United States for support in throwing off Soviet domination. But when Joseph Stalin became mortally ill in March 1953, Eisenhower saw an opportunity for a renewal of the traditional friendship between the Russians and Americans.

Stalin's death climaxed eight years of strained relations. Eisenhower now insisted that Dulles open negotiations with Moscow to bring about peace in Korea. Dulles stalled, determined upon a military victory. Eisenhower grew exasperated.

In April he appealed directly to Stalin's successors, "The new Soviet leadership now has a precious opportunity to . . . help turn the tide of history. Will it do this?"

The Russians responded favorably, and by June a truce was concluded that ended the fighting in Korea. To demonstrate his peaceful intentions further, Eisenhower also slashed military spending by $10 billion in the next two years, despite opposition from the Pentagon.

But the cold war was far from over. American anxiety was fed by Dulles's persistent anti-Soviet policies, and in Congress by Sen. Joseph McCarthy, an ambitious demagogue seeking to advance his career by exploiting anti-Communist hysteria. McCarthy outraged Eisenhower by accusing Gen. George Marshall of having sacrificed American interests to world communism.

Ethel and Julius Rosenberg were executed as Communist spies in June after conviction on dubious evidence for giving atomic bomb "secrets" to the Soviet Union. The Rosenbergs went to their deaths protesting their innocence. Their execution, which provoked world protest, epitomized the tensions and hysteria brought about by the nuclear arms race.

At the beginning of 1954, Dulles, seeking a less expensive but effective way to "contain communism," announced a new foreign policy—"massive retaliation at a time and place of our own choosing"—to deter revolution in various parts of the world. It was a thinly veiled threat to drop atom bombs on either the USSR or Red China, if he deemed it necessary.

Shocked, the Kremlin replied angrily that any attack on the Soviet Union would start a world war that would mean "the death of world civilization." America's NATO allies were appalled at Dulles's brash threat. Intercontinental ballistic missiles had not yet been invented, so that if the Soviet Union were attacked from U.S. overseas bases, atomic reprisals would wipe out NATO countries in West Europe.

Their indignant protests forced Dulles to back down. He explained feebly that he had not meant "turning every local war into world war." But his about-face did little to reassure the Russians about American intentions. They developed a hydrogen bomb six months after the United States detonated one.

Eisenhower offered to meet with Khrushchev to discuss disarmament. Foreign Minister Molotov argued in the Kremlin that all negotiations and cultural and personal contacts with Americans should be avoided as a capitalist snare. But Khrushchev prevailed and agreed to attend a four-power summit conference at Geneva in July 1955.

Eisenhower considered it a hopeful sign when his old friend Marshal Zhukov, suddenly rehabilitated, showed up with the Soviet delegation. The two war comrades enjoyed a private luncheon reunion. At the conference Eisenhower proposed a plan for making sure both sides would live up to the terms of any disarmament treaty. His "open skies" program called for each power to have the right of aerial reconnaissance.

Khrushchev considered overflights of Soviet territory unacceptable because of the opportunity they provided for aerial espionage, but his manner was warm and friendly.

Despite Dulles and Molotov, cultural exchanges began to thaw Soviet-American relations. At Eisenhower's insistence, the State Department began allowing American tourists to visit the Soviet Union again. Supreme Court Justice William O. Douglas, who had been trying in vain to secure a visa for five years, finally won the right to roam Russia as an unofficial goodwill ambassador.

"In Russia, Eisenhower is indeed a great symbol of American friendship," he reported. "That is one reason why the smiles at Geneva had powerful reactions in the villages of Russia, releasing feelings long suppressed. I traveled Russia a month after Geneva and found evidence of friendship for America in every village."

Through an interpreter he gave seminars at various universities, explaining the American way of life. "I always told them the truth," Douglas related, "even when the truth was a minus rather than a plus."

The question most often asked of Douglas was whether the American people desired peace as much as the Russians.

"Both the Russian people and the Russian officials want peace," he reported, adding, "I left Russia with high respect for most of the people I had met. And for many of them I developed a genuine affection."

In February 1956 Khrushchev made it clear that he would like to end the cold war, stabilizing world positions as they were. At the Twentieth Party Congress he proposed a new "coexistence" policy, calling for a Soviet-American treaty to promote mutual understanding and goodwill through increased economic, cultural, and scientific relations.

Eisenhower was quick to respond. "I had long advocated . . . this kind of people-to-people exchange as one fine, progressive step toward peace in the world," he wrote. In September he announced a broad-scale program to encourage private citizens in the arts, education, athletics, law, medicine, and business to organize trips to the Soviet Union.

Touring the country, Chester Bowles reported, "We felt a warmth and friendship which amazed us. On our first night in the USSR in a restaurant in Tashkent, when it became known that we were Americans, the whole room stood up and offered us a toast. This happened again in Samarkand."

Increased Russian-American understanding was advanced by a new agreement which let the Soviet Union publish an English-language monthly, *Soviet Life*, for American distribution, while the United States was permitted to circulate a Russian-language monthly, *Amerika*, in the Soviet Union.

At the same time, however, the CIA continued to encourage revolt in East Europe through Radio Free Europe broadcasts urging the subversion of Communist regimes.

In October student dissatisfaction in Hungary erupted, generating a full-scale uprising against the Budapest government. Leaders of the revolt looked to the West for help, particularly to the United States, but none was forthcoming. Soviet tanks and troops were rushed to Hungary out of fear that the revolt might spread to other East European countries.

This heavy-handed action by the Kremlin produced another chill in Soviet-American relations. The UN voted for an American resolution of censure, fifty-five to eight, and Washington offered asylum to Hungarian "freedom fighters." Moscow bitterly accused Radio Free Europe of having plotted, instigated, and directed "counter-revolution."

In June 1957 U.S. Gen. Lauris Norstad, head of NATO, declared that the West now had the ability to destroy "absolutely" the USSR's ability to make war "in a couple of hours." Khrushchev replied angrily, "Such unreasonable hotheads exist, and we must not forget about them."

He placed on exhibit in Moscow captured U.S. balloons that had been floated over Russia to photograph and map the terrain, and also to drop anti-Soviet propaganda by parachute.

Journalist John Gunther pointed out that if the Russians

had done that to the United States, "there would be a screech of outrage loud enough to rock the Grand Canyon. . . . We would not like it a bit. We might even find ourselves touchy, exasperated, and afraid. . . . Why, the Russians ask, does the United States 'encircle' the Soviet Union with bases, from Okinawa to Morocco, from England to the eastern Mediterranean, if not in preparation for attack?"

Traveling through the Soviet Union late in 1956, Gunther noted that while many Russians feared the American government, they felt that it did not reflect the true feelings of the American people, whom they liked and admired. On public occasions, banners in Red Square proclaimed Russians' desire for "friendship with the American people."   •

★ ☆

On October 4, 1957, the Soviet Union launched a 148-pound satellite named *Sputnik* into orbit around the earth.

The space age had begun. The event stunned the American government and people, shattering all illusions about U.S. technical superiority over the Soviet Union, and creating new fears and apprehension. The shock was doubled less than a month later when a second Sputnik was placed in orbit, this one carrying a live dog as a passenger.

Flustered Republican leaders tried to dismiss Sputnik as just an orbiting "basketball." Speaking for the Democrats, Senate majority leader Lyndon B. Johnson said, "We can no longer consider the Soviet Union to be a nation years behind us in scientific research and industrial ability."

Dr. Edward Teller, creator of the H-bomb, predicted that it would take the United States ten years to catch up. It actually took seven years, during which many Americans felt helpless and frustrated, fearful that the Sputniks could be used as space stations to drop atomic bombs, or to spy out the nation's vital military secrets.

These jitters gave Americans a taste of Russian apprehension caused by U.S. bombers patrolling along the southern borders of the Soviet Union from Turkish air bases. Senator Fulbright noted, "We have treated constant Soviet preoccupation with our overseas bases as sort of an unreasonable Soviet obsession." Now the shoe was on the other foot.

The United States launched a crash program to overtake the Russians in space technology. A new national Aeronautics and Space Administration was created, and given a billion and a half dollars for missile research and production. To create a huge new corps of space scientists, Congress passed the National Defense Education Act.

"The Sputnik was one of the finest things that Russia ever did for us," observed Vannevar Bush, wartime head of U.S. scientific research. "It has waked this country up."

Khrushchev assured Eisenhower that the Soviet Union intended no threat to American security, and wished only for improved relations. On January 27, 1958, both countries signed a formal agreement to cooperate in cultural, educational, technical, and sports fields. Four days later Americans breathed easier when Explorer I, the first American earth satellite, followed Sputnik into orbit.

American pride escalated another notch in April when young concert pianist Van Cliburn of Texas won first prize in the Moscow-sponsored First International Tchaikovsky Competition, a remarkable honor for an American. "His debut," wrote Konstantin Telyatnikov, "aroused more enthusiasm than the conservatory's Grand Hall had heard for a long time . . . a spontaneous response to a wonderful performance."

Similarly, when the Moiseyev Dance Troupe of Moscow opened at New York's Metropolitan Opera House, *Variety* reported, "A dressy crowd of American bourgeoisie yelled, shouted and ran out of expressions of amazement."

Eisenhower wanted to offer a free year in American universities to ten thousand English-speaking Russian students. He was deterred by Dulles, who sought to keep cultural exchanges on a token scale, and by conservative Sen. Barry Goldwater.

The cultural agreement of 1958, nevertheless, was an important step forward in strengthening Soviet-American friendship, and has been renewed regularly every two years since. As a result, American and Russian scientists and specialists of every kind were able to establish continuous contacts and cooperation with each other, with great benefit to the people of both countries.

Khrushchev was anxious to propose a 10 to 15 percent cut in their respective military budgets to Eisenhower, and to conclude the long-delayed peace treaty with Germany, establishing permanent boundaries and the status of Berlin.

He wanted frontiers fixed so that if West Germany violated them, it would be clearly branded the aggressor.

Although the Western Allies had combined their occupation zones of Germany into a West German state, Dulles refused to acknowledge the Russians' right to form an East German state. He demanded reunification, with a reunified Germany rearmed as part of NATO. George Kennan blamed Dulles for refusing to reach a political understanding with the Russians, while forcing them into a dangerous nuclear arms race.

"Until we stop pushing the Kremlin against a closed door," Kennan pointed out, "we shall never learn whether it would be prepared to go through an open door."

Khrushchev noted later, "The United States in those days

refused to make even the most reasonable concessions because John Foster Dulles was still alive. It was he who determined the foreign policy of the United States, not President Eisenhower."

The bankruptcy of the Dulles policy was exposed in July 1958 when marines were rushed to Lebanon on the assumption that the regime was being threatened by outside Communist forces. It soon became embarrassingly obvious that the United States had intervened in a purely internal revolution.

"Mr. President," protested Senator Fulbright, "for years now we have taken the easy way. Let something go wrong—whether it be in China or Nigeria—and we have had a ready answer: The Soviet Union was behind it. What a perfect formula for the evasion of reality and, I may add, what a futile formula. If there is a single factor which . . . explains the predicament in which we now find ourselves, it is our readiness to use the specter of Soviet communism as a cloak for the failure of our own leadership."

When Fulbright became chairman of the Senate Foreign Relations Committee in January 1959, his speeches on American foreign policy caught Khrushchev's attention. They contributed to the Soviet leader's conviction that, despite Dulles, good relations with the American government were possible.

That conviction was strengthened after Dulles's death in May, when Eisenhower replaced him with Christian Herter, but decided to direct foreign policy himself. Next month *New York Times* correspondent Harrison Salisbury reported from Moscow that the Soviet Union was being opened up to American newsmen and tourists, noting "the comparative ease and freedom of conversation and the contacts with Russian people."

The U.S. Academy of Sciences and the USSR Academy of

Sciences reached an agreement in July to exchange information and organize joint forums for scientists of both nations. Out of this cooperation came improved technology in computers, electronics, physics, radioastronomy, laser research, and polymer chemistry. Postgraduate students and researchers began attending each other's institutions of higher learning.

The two countries exchanged expositions. Eisenhower attended the opening of a Soviet exposition in New York City while Khrushchev, accompanied by Vice-president Richard Nixon, attended a preview of the American National Exhibition in Moscow's Sokolniki Park.

Khrushchev was not particularly fond of Nixon, considering him a hostile politician like Joseph McCarthy, who had built his career on attacking communism. "He had been a puppet of McCarthy until McCarthy's star began to fade," Khrushchev wrote later, "at which point Nixon turned his back on him. So he was an unprincipled puppet, which is the most dangerous kind."

The two men exchanged sharp words in the Kremlin over a "Captive Nations" resolution of sympathy passed by Congress to criticize Soviet control of East Europe. Khrushchev considered the timing of it a calculated affront.

The note of acrimony continued when he and Nixon visited the American exhibition, which featured a typical suburban home. In front of TV cameras in a model kitchen, they waged an impromptu debate as a hundred or so workmen gathered around to listen. Nixon bragged that the average weekly wage of an American worker was as much as a skilled Soviet worker earned in a month, and that he could buy on time payments a house, TV set, and car similar to those exhibited. Moreover, American workers were free to speak their minds.

"You are showing here your house and your kitchen, and

hope to make the Soviet people marvel," Khrushchev snapped. "To buy such a house an American must have very many dollars. . . . You speak much of your freedom—which includes freedom to spend the night under a bridge!"

Nixon pointed his finger at Khrushchev and said sternly, "Mr. Khrushchev, you don't know everything!" Russian observers gasped at this affront to the Soviet premier. But Khrushchev's determination to achieve détente with the United States remained unshaken. He promptly accepted an invitation from Eisenhower to visit the United States.

A shrewd showman, Khrushchev scored his own propaganda points for the Soviet Union by landing a rocket on the moon just three days before his arrival in Washington on September 15, accompanied by his English-speaking wife. He presented the president with a model of Lunik II as a gift.

As a matter of principle, Khrushchev refused to wear formal dress or a tuxedo to the White House dinner in his honor. "These, in Communist eyes, were symbols of capitalism," Eisenhower noted. Khrushchev told the president that he had come to Washington hopeful of reaching an agreement assuring Soviet-American peace. Eisenhower agreed that there was "no future in mutual suicide." There would have to be greater trust between the two governments, Khrushchev said. He protested a recent anti-Communist speech by Nixon as inflammatory.

"After having read that speech," Khrushchev told the president, "I am surprised to find on arriving here that people in the United States welcome us with such tolerance and obvious friendliness." He added, "In the Soviet Union there would have been no welcome whatsoever if I had, in advance, publicly spoken against the visitor."

"That," Eisenhower replied dryly, "is the basic difference between our two systems."

Khrushchev was suspicious when offered a tour of Washington in a helicopter. He declined until he learned that Eisenhower intended to accompany him. "Oh, if you are to be in the same helicopter," he decided, "of course I will go!"

At the state dinner he declared, "We believe our system to be better—and you believe yours to be better. But surely we should not bring quarrels out into the arena of open struggle. Let history judge which of us is right. . . . What we should do now is to strive together to improve our relations. We need nothing from the United States, and you need nothing that we have. It is true that you are richer than we are at present. But then tomorrow we will be as rich as you are, and the day after tomorrow . . . even richer."

When Khrushchev prepared to set off on a ten-day tour of the country, he both fascinated and angered Americans by his abrasive, ebullient manner. Forbidden to visit Disneyland for fear of exposing him to a crackpot attack, he scoffed, "Is that where you have your rocket-launching pads?" Shown a huge Iowa farm, he insisted that Soviet agricultural methods were more advanced. But Lyndon Johnson indicated that he was far more impressed than he would admit: "That Iowa farm that Khrushchev saw damn near upset the whole Communist system."

Meeting Johnson, Khrushchev snapped, "I know all about you. I have read all your speeches and I don't like *any* of them." The Soviet leader was incensed at a dinner in San Francisco when conservative labor leaders attacked him more virulently than any American capitalist he had met.

Returning east, Khrushchev was invited by Eisenhower

to Camp David for a three-day visit. Still suspicious, he wondered whether Camp David might be a detention camp. "I can laugh about it now," he wrote later, "but I'm a little bit ashamed. It shows how ignorant we were in some respects."

At Camp David, asked his impressions of the United States, Khrushchev told Eisenhower that he was not impressed by American prosperity. So large a number of individual homes represented an extravagant method of housing, and so many millions of cars reflected a waste of money, effort, and time.

"Your people do not seem to like the place where they live," he pointed out, "and always want to be on the move going someplace else." Russians, he said, were more contented.

The two leaders discussed military spending.

"My military leaders come to me," Eisenhower told Khrushchev, "and say, 'Mr. President, we need such and such a sum for such and such a program.' I say, 'Sorry, we don't have the funds.' They say, 'We have reliable information that the Soviet Union has already allocated funds for their own such program.' . . . . So I give in. That's how they wring money out of me. . . . Now tell me, how is it with you?"

"It's just the same!" Khrushchev exclaimed.

"We really should come to some sort of an agreement in order to stop this fruitless, really wasteful rivalry."

They agreed to hold a summit in Paris in the spring.

"The ice of the Cold War has not only cracked but begun to melt," Khrushchev assured American newsmen. Returning home, he told the Politburo that the responsible leaders of America were opposed to war, and that Eisenhower was reasonable and farsighted. He had hopes of settling their differences over Germany at the Paris summit conference.

Nevertheless, Eisenhower did not object when the Pentagon sent new high-flying U-2 spy planes on photo reconnaissance flights clear across the Soviet Union. He was assured that if anything went wrong, the plane was programmed to disintegrate, so that it would be impossible for either its equipment or its pilot to fall into Soviet hands.

The first overflight was made April 9, 1960. There is evidence that Khrushchev was made aware of it, but decided to say nothing publicly because he was anxious not to dampen the spirit of Camp David less than a month before the scheduled Paris summit. On May 2 a second overflight was undertaken because the Pentagon was worried that agreements reached at the conference might ground the U-2 spy planes.

The second U-2, flown by pilot Francis Gary Powers, was shot down deep over Soviet territory. Powers parachuted to earth, failing to use the suicide needle supplied to CIA agents on high-risk missions. The plane failed to self-destruct. Both were captured by the Russians.

To make matters worse, next day the House of Representatives, unaware of the U-2 disaster, adopted a resolution calling for "liberation" of East Europe and even some parts of the Soviet Union.

Khrushchev was understandably upset. On May 5, during a speech to the Supreme Soviet, he revealed the bare fact that an American U-2 plane had been shot down over Russian soil, but implied that it might have been sent by "Pentagon militarists" without Eisenhower's knowledge. It was an attempt to offer the president a graceful way out of the dilemma.

The State Department hastily announced that an

unarmed weather research plane had been missing since May 1, and might have accidentally strayed over Soviet air space.

Two days later Khrushchev told the Supreme Soviet, "Comrades, I must let you into a secret. When I made my report I deliberately refrained from mentioning that the pilot was alive and healthy." Powers had confessed that he was a CIA agent, and had been collecting espionage information by photographing Soviet airfields.

Caught in a lie, the State Department now admitted that the Russians were correct, but insisted that the flight had been unauthorized by Washington. Eisenhower, sensitive to the humiliating implication that such important decisions were made without his knowledge, felt compelled to brand this second excuse a lie as well. He acknowledged personal responsibility for the U-2 overflight.

The president's public admission made Khrushchev disappointed and angry. He had built up Eisenhower to the Russian people as his great friend and a man of peace. Soviet critics berated Khrushchev for having been gullible.

When the summit conference opened in Paris on May 16, he denounced the American government for its "provocative act" and "treacherous nature." He demanded that Eisenhower apologize, promise to discontinue any more U-2 flights over Russia, and punish those who had organized them. He also publicly canceled his invitation to the president to visit the Soviet Union, declaring angrily, "The Russian people would say I was mad to welcome a man who sends spy planes over here."

Stunned, Eisenhower refused to apologize. The summit conference was shattered before it had even begun. Khrushchev stalked out, indicating that he would renew his attempts at détente in another six months, when a new administration would be in power in Washington.

"The big error we made was, of course, in the issuance of a premature and erroneous cover story," Eisenhower admitted later. "Allowing myself to be persuaded on this score is my principal personal regret—except for the U-2 failure itself—regarding the whole affair."

"It seems incredible," observed Soviet expert Fred Warner Neal, "that the May U-2 flight was permitted on the eve of a summit meeting at which, presumably, we were going to discuss possible settlements with the Soviet Union. But regardless of the unfortunate timing, the ever-suspicious Russians were bound to read in it aggressive . . . intent."

Walter Lippmann called Eisenhower's refusal to take the way out Khrushchev had offered him by denying responsibility and apologizing as "a fatal error . . . an irreparable mistake." Khrushchev agreed, stating, "That is when it became obvious that the purpose of the aggressive actions by the United States was to torpedo the summit meeting." But the president's defenders argued that this was Khrushchev's intention, and that the U-2 had simply given him a good excuse.

Matters were not helped in July when two American RB-47 fliers flew too close to the USSR's Arctic shore, and were shot down and captured. Soviet-American relations turned even chillier, raising fears that the U-2 and RB-47 incidents might escalate the nuclear arms race.

Gen. Nikolai A. Talensky, Soviet general staff expert, warned that in the event of thermonuclear war, "not a single country would escape the ensuing crushing, devastating blows. . . . The world population would be reduced by one half. . . . Moreover, the most active, capable, and civilized portion would be wiped out."

★ ☆

Americans grew alarmed when Khrushchev, in an exchange with an American correspondent, was quoted as threatening, "We will bury you!" He later insisted that his words had been distorted. "We, the Soviet Union, weren't going to bury anyone," he explained. "The working class of the United States would bury its enemy the bourgeois class of the United States."

At the opening of the UN session in September 1960, he returned to the United States as chairman of the Soviet delegation in order to denounce American foreign policy. When his movements were restricted to Manhattan and Long Island, he held a news conference from the balcony of the Soviet embassy on Park Avenue, quipping, "I'm under house arrest."

At the UN he denounced Secretary Dag Hammarskjold for "pro-Western bias." When Hammarskjold began to reply, Khrushchev overplayed his hand by removing a shoe and banging it on the desk to drown out the secretary's address. UN delegates were shocked by this breach of diplomatic etiquette, and Soviet officials were embarrassed. This gaffe was thought to be one factor that subsequently contributed to his downfall.

In 1960, when Senator John F. Kennedy challenged Vice-president Richard Nixon for the White House, Khrushchev felt that a victory by Nixon would doom any chance for a Soviet-American rapprochement. Harriman privately asked the Russian leader to say equally harsh things about Kennedy as he did about Nixon, so that Kennedy could not be accused of being "soft on communism," Nixon's favorite political smear.

Khrushchev obliged, and also rejected Eisenhower's

request shortly before election that he release the two U.S. airmen shot down over Arctic Russia as a goodwill gesture. Had he done so, Khrushchev later told Kennedy's secretary of the interior, Stewart Udall, Nixon might have been the beneficiary by as much as half a million votes. "So I decided to wait," he explained. "Maybe that was the little drop that made the difference in your close election?"

In a congratulatory cable to Kennedy, Khrushchev declared, "We are ready to develop the most friendly relations between the Soviet and the American peoples. . . . We are convinced that there are no insurmountable obstacles to the preservation and consolidation of peace."

"Let us negotiate," Kennedy told Americans in his inaugural address, "not out of fear, but let us not fear to negotiate." In his state of the union message he invited the Soviet Union "to join with us in developing a weather prediction program, in a new communications satellite program, and in preparations for probing the distant planets of Mars and Venus."

Khrushchev demonstrated Soviet goodwill by releasing the two RB-147 fliers. He also sent disarmament experts to meet their American opposite numbers informally at a new Pugwash Conference called by Cyrus Eaton in Nova Scotia.

Seeking to "de-emotionalize the Cold War at home," Kennedy instructed American admirals and generals to tone down their anti-Soviet exhortations. He also ended post office censorship of Soviet publications in the U.S. mails, and lifted a ban on the importation of Russian crabmeat.

In April 1961 the Soviet Union sent an astronaut, Maj. Uri Gagarin, into space for an orbit of the globe, and brought him safely to earth. It was a scientific feat of the first magnitude, winning the applause of the world. In the United States admiration was mixed with chagrin.

"Do we have a chance of beating the Soviets . . . to the moon and back with a man?" Kennedy asked his vice-president, Lyndon B. Johnson. As chairman of the new Space Council, Johnson reported a consensus that the United States did.

On April 17 Kennedy made his first serious mistake. He permitted the CIA to go ahead with a secret plan, evolved under the Eisenhower administration, to help Cuban exiles invade the Bay of Pigs in Cuba in an attempt to overthrow the revolutionary government of Fidel Castro.

The Castro regime turned to the Soviet Union for aid and protection. Khrushchev sent an angry note to Washington denouncing the invasion, and pledging "all necessary assistance" to Cuba. But it proved unnecessary. The invaders, armed and transported by the CIA, found no support in Cuba, and were easily defeated on the beaches. Afterwards Kennedy gloomily asked Senator Fulbright, "How could I have agreed to such a stupid mistake?"

He now paid more attention to the advice of liberals like Fulbright, Adlai Stevenson, Averell Harriman, George Kennan, Chester Bowles, John Kenneth Galbraith, and Mike Mansfield. In their view, the cold war myth of a worldwide "Communist monolith" had badly misled American foreign policy, which required a political program, not a military one.

Agreeing that it was time for a new approach, Kennedy arranged to meet Khrushchev in Vienna to discuss Soviet-American differences. At their meeting in June, sixty-seven-year-old Khrushchev contrasted the USSR and the United States as young and old nations. The forty-three-year-old Kennedy smiled, "If you'll look across the table, you'll see that we're not so old."

Khrushchev expressed the hope that Kennedy was

prepared to accept a coexistence policy. Kennedy expressed admiration for the economic and scientific accomplishments of the USSR, but asked if Khrushchev appreciated the importance of not encouraging communism in areas of the world vital to Western interests.

Khrushchev countered that mutual trust could not be developed if the Americans continued to suspect that whenever there was a revolution, Moscow had manufactured it. The United States, he pointed out, was provoking revolutions by backing reactionary governments, as it had in Iran and the Cuba of Batista. Castro, in fact, had not been a Communist, but the Bay of Pigs invasion had made him into one.

Kennedy reminded the Soviet premier that he had pledged support for all wars of "national liberation." Wasn't that interference in other nations' affairs? Khrushchev replied that the United States, which had waged its own revolution against Britain, ought not to deny the same right to other oppressed peoples. Washington had taken sixteen years to recognize the Russian Revolution, and after thirteen years it still did not recognize the Chinese Revolution.

Their discussion grew acrimonious when it turned to the problem of Berlin. Khrushchev complained that there was still no peace settlement in Germany, sixteen years after the end of World War II. Instead, a rearmed West Germany was now a partner in NATO. "West Berlin is a bone that must come out of the Soviet throat," Khrushchev insisted. Unless a treaty was agreed upon soon, the USSR would sign its own treaty with East Germany in December. That would automatically cancel all occupation rights in Berlin.

The United States would then have to negotiate access to the city, not with the USSR, but with East Germany. If the

Americans sought to violate East German borders forcibly, force would be met by force. "I want peace," Khrushchev said, "but if you want war, that is your problem."

"It is you, and not I, who wants to force a change," Kennedy replied. He added grimly, "It will be a cold winter."

New York Times correspondent James Reston, talking to the president afterwards, found him shaken by Khrushchev's unexpected verbal assault. "I think he did it because of the Bay of Pigs," Kennedy mused. "I think he thought that anyone who was so young and inexperienced as to get into that mess could be taken, and anyone who got into it, and didn't see it through, had no guts. So he just beat hell out of me. So I've got a terrible problem. . . . Until we remove those ideas we won't get anywhere with him. So we have to act."

Kennedy's conclusion had important consequences. His determination to show Khrushchev that he could be tough led him to risk a nuclear world war in the Cuban missile crisis. It also led him to send fifteen thousand American military advisers and Green Berets to Vietnam, to wage counterrevolutionary warfare against the Communist regime of Ho Chi Minh.

★ ☆

On August 13 East Berlin began constructing a wall separating East from West Berlin. As tension mounted in the city, Khrushchev canceled cuts in the Soviet military budget and resumed testing a series of nuclear weapons.

Meanwhile, under the Soviet-American cultural agreement, more and more American journalists were exploring Russian life after forty-four years of Communist government. Mervyn Jones reported in his book *The Antagonists* that Russians paid only 25 percent as much as Americans for books and records, 10 percent as much for haircuts, 12 to 33 percent as much for rent. Clothing and manufactured items were much more expensive, however, and of lesser quality with limited choices.

Jones was impressed with the number of women in the professions—two-thirds of Soviet doctors, most teachers, many office administrators, judges, and prosecutors. Women were also street cleaners, janitors, and hod carriers. Soviet women were critical of American wives who stayed home.

Benjamin Appel reported in his book *With Many Voices* that Russians expressed warm feelings toward the American people, considering any difficulties in U.S.–USSR relations the fault of politicians on both sides. They were incredulous that Americans could fear the Soviet Union and most were critical of both Soviet and American nuclear tests, and wanted them stopped.

Exchanges of performers helped increase Soviet-American goodwill. Benny Goodman and his jazz ensemble toured the USSR. The New York City Ballet gave fifty-five performances to overflow houses in Moscow, Leningrad, and other cities.

In a cultural exchange of poets, Robert Frost, eighty-eight, was asked by President Kennedy to go to the Soviet Union as a goodwill ambassador.

Frost was welcomed to the Soviet Union by a delegation of Soviet writers, including two who had translated his poems into Russian over thirty years earlier. Asked if he wouldn't find communication difficult because of the language barrier, he replied, "We all laugh in the same language."

In a talk with Khrushchev, Frost urged a "noble rivalry" between Americans and Russians, rather than hostile conflict.

"I found the Russians a great people," he reported, "good-natured in their confidence that peaceful coexistence . . . might be a better way than war . . . to win the ultimate victory for the workers of the world. I found them as determined to beat us as I think we are to beat them in sports, in art, in science, in business, in democracy, in chivalry and magnanimity."

Cooperation, rather than competition, was stressed by Russian and American scientists. The American research vessel *Chain* and the Soviet research ship *Mikhail Lomonsov* began working together in the Atlantic on oceanography projects. The USSR Academy of Sciences and NASA prepared to coordinate peaceful studies of outer space. Soviet and American doctors exchanged papers on the unique work both were doing in the transplantation of human organs.

Although Soviet-American relations appeared to be making good progress on the people-to-people level, diplomatic relations took a sharp turn for the worse when Khrushchev decided to respond to Castro's plea for protection by sending Soviet missiles secretly to Cuba in 1962. This did little to alter the two-to-one American superiority over the USSR in missiles, but discovery of the move alarmed Americans. The Russians insisted that the missiles were intended purely for Cuban defense, in case the CIA tried another Bay of Pigs invasion.

For ten days Kennedy held agonized meetings with his cabinet, trying to decide what to do while the missiles were being installed on launching pads less than ninety miles from Florida. Angry hawks wanted an aerial strike to knock them out, even at the risk of nuclear war with the USSR. Doves urged patience and negotiations with the Russians.

Replying to the American protest, Khrushchev declared, "The whole world knows that the United States of America is ringing the Soviet Union and other Socialist countries with bases. . . . When measures are nevertheless taken to strengthen the defenses of this or that country, the United States raises an outcry and declares that an attack . . . is being prepared against them. What conceit!"

American hawks demanded a naval blockade of Cuba until Khrushchev agreed to remove the missiles. Vice-president Lyndon Johnson warned, "Stopping a Russian ship is an act of war. . . . Some people have more guts than brains." But Kennedy finally decided that a blockade was a compromise solution that would put peace or war squarely up to Khrushchev.

On October 20, 1962, the world held its breath as twenty-five Russian ships steaming toward Havana held their course, while ninety ships of the American fleet and eight aircraft carriers moved into position to intercept and search them for missiles.

Kennedy warned Moscow that even one missile launched from Cuba, against any nation in the Western Hemisphere, would be regarded by the United States as an attack by the Soviet Union, and would be met by a full-scale counterattack.

Historian Richard Walton observed that Kennedy's "decision to go to the brink of nuclear war was irresponsible and reckless to a supreme degree," that it "risked the kind of terrible miscalculation that Kennedy was always warning Khrushchev about," that it was "unnecessary." For one thing, President Osvaldo Dorticas of Cuba, with Castro's approval, had already indicated that "our weapons would be unnecessary" if the United States pledged no further attacks on Cuba.

The world waited in dread of news that the Russian and American ships had met and shots had been fired, touching off nuclear warfare. After terrible suspense it was learned

159

that Khrushchev had ordered some Soviet ships to turn back, and others to submit peacefully to American inspection.

On October 26 Khrushchev sent a secret message to Kennedy expressing alarm over the risk of nuclear war, and asking for assurances that the United States would not invade Cuba. Next day another message came through a different channel, offering to remove the Russian missiles from Cuba if the United States agreed to dismantle its military bases in Turkey.

The president's brother, Atty. Gen. Robert Kennedy, suggested that they ignore the second message and reply quickly to the first one, pledging not to invade Cuba if Khrushchev agreed to remove the Soviet missiles. When the president followed this advice, Khrushchev was satisfied and the crisis was over. The blockade was lifted, the missiles were withdrawn, and the whole world breathed more easily.

"Both sides showed that if the desire to avoid war is strong enough," Khrushchev declared, "even the most pressing dispute can be solved by compromise." Kennedy praised the Soviet Premier's contribution to the cause of peace. U.S. missiles were later removed from Turkey.

In June 1963 Kennedy made an important speech at American University, seeking to end cold war prejudices on both sides once and for all. He reminded Americans that the Russians had even more reason to hate war than they did: "No nation in the history of battle ever suffered more than the Soviet Union suffered in the course of the Second World War."

In a nuclear age, peace had become "the necessary rational end of rational men." An important first step toward world peace and disarmament, Kennedy urged, would be a nuclear test ban treaty to stop the poisoning of the earth's atmosphere with radioactive fallout.

Khrushchev agreed to nuclear test ban talks, and began to prepare the way by defusing cold war sentiment among the Communist nations of the world.

"Comrades," he told one international gathering, "we want the question of who wins out on the world scale not to be decided by a war between states. The system that gives people more freedom, that gives people more material and cultural goods, is the system that will ultimately triumph."

On August 5, 1963, the United States, the Soviet Union, and Great Britain signed a treaty outlawing nuclear testing in the atmosphere, in outer space, and under the water, and placing limitations on underground testing.

Soviet Foreign Minister Andrei Gromyko warned Peking against any warlike moves: "The two greatest modern powers have left far behind any other country in the world. If they unite for peace, there can be no war. If any madman wants to go to war, we have but to shake our fingers to warn them off."

As a practical expression of the new understanding between Moscow and Washington, a special teletype circuit—"the hot line"—was installed on August 30 between the White House and the Kremlin. It provided instant communication between the two heads of government in case of emergency, reducing the possibility that a nuclear war could be triggered by accident or misunderstanding.

The Russians were stunned when John F. Kennedy was assassinated on November 21, 1963, by Lee Harvey Oswald. Ironically, Oswald had lived in the Soviet Union for a while, returning to the United States with a Russian wife. Wild rumors that he was a Soviet agent were quickly dispelled by an FBI revelation that he had been denied

Russian citizenship as an undesirable ne'er-do-well, and had left the USSR disenchanted.

In Moscow Khrushchev was the first to sign a condolence book signed by thousands of Russians. Soviet TV reported the funeral, including church services, and Russian radio played funeral dirges in honor of the late president's memory.

Lyndon B. Johnson sought to continue Kennedy's understanding with the Russians. Before he could arrange a summit conference with Khrushchev, the Soviet leader was suddenly ousted from power. The chief reason for his downfall was the explosion of an atom bomb by Red China. Khrushchev was blamed for having permitted the split with Peking, which was now not only hostile toward Russia but would soon have nuclear weapons on the Sino-Soviet border. This new threat made Khrushchev's successors, party chairman Leonid Brezhnev and Premier Aleksei Kosygin, even more anxious than Khrushchev to draw closer to the United States in friendship and security pacts.

Soviet-American understanding struck another snag in the Vietnam War. After the Second World War, Communist patriot Ho Chi Minh had led a revolution against French colonialism in Vietnam. His regime at Hanoi in the North had forced the French to sue for peace at Geneva, where a treaty provided for national elections. But Dulles had sabotaged the elections through a puppet regime at Saigon in the South.

American military supplies and money had poured into Saigon, preventing unification. Ho Chi Minh had appealed to the Soviet Union and Red China for equal assistance. Kennedy had sent fifteen thousand "advisers" to South Vietnam, a move which Johnson chose to regard as an "American commitment." Deciding that American prestige required a military victory, in February 1965 Johnson ordered continuous U.S. bombing of North Vietnam by air and sea forces.

When the bombing failed to crush North Vietnam, and South Vietnamese troops showed no desire to fight for the corrupt Saigon regime, Johnson intervened in the civil war with half a million American troops. Moscow and Peking sent Hanoi money and supplies, but no military forces.

Brezhnev and Kosygin warned Johnson that there could be no significant improvement in U.S.-USSR relations as long as American aggression in Vietnam continued. They wanted to bring about some kind of political settlement, but could not do so openly for fear of laying themselves open to Red Chinese charges of "appeasing Wall Street imperialism."

The Pentagon did not help matters by directing American bombing missions against Hanoi during a visit there by Kosygin. The Russians angrily canceled a track and field meet for Soviet and American athletes, and rerouted an American jazz group away from major Soviet cities.

Chicago priest Harold M. Koch was so outraged by the American intervention in Vietnam that he sought political asylum in the Soviet Union. From Moscow he warned fellow Americans that persistence in the war could lead to totalitarianism.

Father Koch was shocked when the Ministry of Foreign Affairs, which had asked him to write an article on the danger of fascism in America, insisted that he change it to state that the United States had already turned Fascist. Refusing to exaggerate the true state of affairs, he asked for an exit visa and continued opposing the war from Sweden.

In the fall of 1966 Johnson held out an olive branch to Moscow by announcing that he was removing a ban on exports of hundreds of American products to Russia and

East Europe, while offering generous terms for trade. He also invited talks with the Russians about mutual reduction of their armed forces in Europe, reassuring them that the United States had no intention of letting West Germany have any nuclear weapons.

Despite Vietnam, after a series of talks with Johnson and Secretary of State Dean Rusk, Gromyko took steps to warm up the Soviet-American climate. The American and Russian delegations at the UN worked out plans for a nuclear nonproliferation treaty, binding all nations signing it to prevent the spread of nuclear weapons to nations which did not already have them. As a goodwill gesture, the Russians released a U.S. peace corpsman stationed in Iran who had been found illegally on the Soviet side of the border.

In December both nations negotiated a "Treaty on Principles Governing the Activities of States in the Exploration and Use of Outer Space, Including the Moon and Other Celestial Bodies," foreshadowing the joint flight in space less than a decade later by Soviet and American astronauts.

In January 1967 Johnson wrote Kosygin proposing to end the arms race. Kosygin accepted his invitation to Glassboro, New Jersey, for a summit conference.

The Glassboro summit warmed relations to the point that both leaders now began to consult each other about pressing world problems that threatened the peace. During the Arab-Israeli six-day war of 1967, they used the hot line twenty-seven times.

On June 8 Johnson received word that a U.S. Navy ship had been torpedoed off the Sinai coast, killing ten men and wounding a hundred. The ship had been attacked in error by Israeli gunboats and planes. Promptly dispatching an aircraft carrier to investigate, Johnson used the hot line to inform Kosygin, so that the Russians would not misunderstand the approach of a U.S. carrier to Egypt.

Kosygin agreed to inform "the proper parties." Johnson's notification greatly impressed the Russians. "Use of the hot line for this purpose, to prevent misunderstanding," declared the president, "was exactly what both parties had envisioned." Kosygin said later that it helped them accomplish "more on . . . one day than others could accomplish in three years."

Johnson found the Vietnam War a serious domestic problem as increasing numbers of American youths demonstrated against it. Many refused to be drafted, and went to jail or fled abroad. The desertion rate was high among those who went to Vietnam and were appalled by the corruption of the Saigon regime.

The Soviet Union was also having some difficulties with dissident Russian youths. The Communist party journal *Kommunist Vooruzhennikh Sil* complained that some Russian young people were pacifists, and lacked the hatred many of the older generation held for the Soviet Union's enemies.

When Joseph Stalin's daughter, Svetlana Alliluyeva, defected to the United States from India, *New York Times* columnist Brooks Atkinson observed that her defection was undoubtedly painful to all patriotic Russians.

In 1967 the United States and USSR agreed to initiate direct, reciprocal air services between New York and Moscow. They also signed a treaty increasing the number of consulates in each nation, in effect opening up each other's country for more wide-ranging travel, trade, and cultural relations.

An American Study Mission spent the early summer of 1968 traveling through the Soviet Union, and met in Moscow with members of the Union of Soviet Journalists to discuss the role of the press.

While they stressed the importance of freedom of the press, the Russians emphasized its social responsibility. *Pravda* foreign correspondent Serguei N. Vichnevski admitted that the Russian press didn't criticize the Soviet system, but pointed out that American papers almost never challenged the basic premise of capitalism. Some criticism might be expressed of its shortcomings, but not of the system itself.

The American mission was surprised to learn that the satirical columns of Art Buchwald were often reprinted in the Soviet press, and were highly popular. It was a shame, Vichnevski said, that the USSR had no Buchwald, because someone with his incisive humor was greatly needed. Whether a Soviet Buchwald would have been tolerated was a moot question.

The Johnson-Kosygin Glassboro summit produced results.

"If July 1, 1968, figures in the history books of the future, it will be because of what happened that morning in the East Room of the White House," Johnson wrote. "A few minutes after 11:30 A.M., in that gold-draped room, before hundreds of witnesses and in the glare of television floodlights, representatives of the Soviet Union, the United Kingdom, the United States, and more than fifty other nations signed the Treaty on the Nonproliferation of Nuclear Weapons."

Nations without a nuclear capability pledged not to try to make or receive such weapons from others. They were assured, in turn, of access to nuclear power for peaceful purposes. Nuclear nations promised to negotiate arms control and disarmament. The United States and the USSR also agreed to put no nuclear weapons into orbit around the earth. The new treaty laid the foundation for future Strategic Arms Limitation Treaty (SALT) talks to limit nuclear arms.

"I expected no miracles in terms of U.S.-Soviet relations during my presidency," Johnson declared, "but I felt strongly that the two most powerful nations in the world had several things in common—above all, the need to avoid confrontations that could lead to disaster for all mankind as well as for each other."

Forced to drop his bid for reelection because of the unpopular Vietnam War, Johnson was anxious to leave office with a redeeming accomplishment by getting the SALT talks under way. In August he asked for a new summit with Kosygin in Moscow, and the Soviet leader readily agreed.

Before it could be held, however, a revolt occurred against the Communist government of Czechoslovakia, and the Soviet Union sent tanks and troops to suppress it. Ambassador Dobrynin paid an urgent call at the White House to tell Johnson that the action did not involve U.S. interests and "should not harm the Soviet-American relations," which Moscow wished to continue improving. But Johnson, pressured by America's NATO allies, felt compelled to advise Kosygin that their summit would have to be postponed until Soviet troops were no longer garrisoned in Czechoslovakia.

The Kremlin grew cool, feeling that East Europe was none of Washington's business, particularly since Russian Intelligence reports blamed the uprising in Czechoslovakia on an influx of some fifteen hundred CIA agents into Prague.

American anti-Vietnam dissenters were disappointed by

the Soviet intervention in Czechoslovakia, and also by the exile of five Russian dissenters who demonstrated in protest in Red Square. Bruce Nelson, a young American draft resister from San Francisco, asked a conference of the Soviet Peace [in Vietnam] Committee if the Russians would join in worldwide amnesty for all war resisters, including the Moscow Five.

Professor O. S. Kharkhardin of the Institute of International Relations replied that the Moscow Five were "idlers and parasites" who "got less than they deserved." Conference committee chairman Yuri Zukhov ruled Czechoslovakia a "nonitem" for discussion by the conferees, despite pressure from the American delegation to put it on the agenda.

Late in the year the Russians proposed new talks to settle problems of Vietnam, peace in the Middle East, and arms limitation. But it was too late for the Johnson administration; Richard Nixon, the anti-Communist hard-liner, would shortly enter the White House.

Ironically, it was his administration which would now inherit the opportunity to end the cold war once and for all, and restore traditional Soviet-American friendship.

PART V

★ ☆

BREAKTHROUGH TO DÉTENTE
1972

Foreign policy decisions were turned over to the new president's adviser, Henry Kissinger, who was convinced that American interests required world stability, not cold war. Both the Soviet Union and Red China wished to be on good terms with the United States, because each Communist rival feared that the other would form a separate alliance with Washington.

At Nixon's first presidential news conference, he retreated from his campaign cry for "clear-cut military superiority" over the Soviet Union. Now, cued by Kissinger, he called only for a "sufficiency" of military power. He proposed arms-control talks with the Russians "in a way that will promote progress on outstanding political problems at the same time."

In July 1969 Soviet Foreign Minister Gromyko told the Supreme Soviet, "We took note of President Nixon's statement that, in his opinion, a period of confrontation is followed by an era of talks. The Soviet Union stands for talks. If the U.S. Government continues to follow this line in practice, we are willing to find agreement with the United States on mutual and world problems."

Kissinger at once undertook negotiations which led in November to the opening of the SALT talks in Helsinki to limit the strategic arms race.

"We are moving . . . from an era of confrontation to an era of negotiation," Nixon said in his 1970 state of the union address.

There was also political purpose in Nixon's moving toward détente with the Russians. His reelection in 1972 would be jeopardized if American troops were still fighting in Vietnam. Kissinger sought to persuade the Russians to use their influence with Hanoi to get North Vietnam to agree to a political settlement that would end the war, without Nixon's seeming to have suffered a military defeat. A slow but gradual withdrawal of U.S. forces from Vietnam during the first Nixon administration gave the Russians an excuse for urging Hanoi to reach an accommodation with Kissinger.

In the new climate of Soviet-American goodwill, Moscow held open house for increasing numbers of U.S. visitors as diversified as Hubert Humphrey, Arthur Goldberg, and Kirk Douglas. Astronaut Frank Borman came to Moscow to help arrange publication of a joint Soviet-American book on space biology and medicine, while Soviet cosmonauts in Siberia played host to U.S. astronaut Neil Armstrong.

In January 1971 representatives of NASA and the USSR Academy of Sciences worked out plans to cooperate in the exploration and use of outer space, including the linkup of manned American and Russian spaceships, and manned orbiting laboratories. They also agreed to swap samples of lunar soil. By the end of the year both nations had put artificial satellites around Mars, designed to function in cooperation with an exchange of discoveries between U.S. and USSR scientists.

Lessening tensions made possible Alaska Airlines'

inauguration of the first commercial flights from the United States to the Soviet Union, via Siberia. In 1970 and 1971 over twenty thousand American scientists, engineers, agriculturists, teachers, businessmen, and politicians made professional trips to visit their Soviet counterparts.

American and Soviet gymnasts competed in a 1971 tournament at Riga. Some of the Americans won awards and high praise from Russian champions for the intricacy and beauty of their movements. "There's no longer the big gap there was ten years ago," observed Larissa Latynina, "between Soviet and American gymnastic standards."

American opera singer Mary Costa toured the Soviet Union in *Faust* and *La Traviata*. She was vastly impressed by the Soviet guarantee of employment for theatrical artists. "They are confident of their position until they retire," she observed. "This makes it possible for them to concentrate completely on creation." She found Russian opera audiences enormously appreciative when they enjoyed a performance.

When the Young Presidents, an American business organization, toured seven Soviet cities to study the Russian economy, Oscar Gerber reported, "Now we know that most people in the United States have wrong ideas about what is going on in the Soviet Union. My own greatest impression is surprise. I was surprised by everything I saw."

So were state governors who toured the Soviet Union.

"The progress we saw everywhere in the fields of housing and transportation, education and planning was most impressive," said Gov. Dale Bumpers of Arkansas.

Gov. Louis Ferré of Puerto Rico said, "Their intelligent and far-reaching vision in planning their cities to make them livable and efficient is an approach that can be used elsewhere to face the urban crisis that menaces the world."

Kissinger's negotiations with the Russians were enormously successful. On May 22, 1972 Nixon flew to Moscow for a summit meeting with Brezhnev. One week later a fascinated world watched on TV sets as the two leaders signed a formal treaty creating a sweeping partnership between Communist Russia and capitalist America in wide fields of endeavor.

Détente marked an official end to the cold war. Dangerous rivalry between the earth's two superpowers had been transformed into a new era of peaceful cooperation.

Both sides agreed to limit their missile systems proportionately, and to avoid military confrontations that could possibly lead to nuclear war. A naval and aircraft agreement set out joint rules of procedure that would prevent incidents between Soviet and American forces on and over the sea.

Separate and wide-ranging agreements were signed providing for joint research and cooperation between both nations' experts in the fields of science, engineering, medicine and public health, peaceful uses of nuclear energy, environmental protection, earthquake prediction, exploration and use of outer space, trade relations, education, and the arts.

A Soviet trade delegation flew to Washington to open negotiations with business and banking leaders in New York and Chicago. The result was a new commercial agreement to end discriminatory tariffs against each other's goods, and grant each other "most favored nation" treatment. The U.S. Export-Import Bank arranged long-term credits to finance large Soviet purchases of American machinery and equipment.

During 1972 trade between the two countries tripled.

Capitalist sales to a socialist economy were not without problems, however. When the Soviet Union, experiencing crop shortages, bought over a billion dollars' worth of American wheat, huge profits were made by America's agricultural middlemen, rather than the wheat farmers. The sale also caused shortages at home, driving up American prices for bread and flour. An angry outcry forced Secretary of Agriculture Earl Butz to promise that future wheat exports would be carefully controlled.

Armand Hammer, the first American businessman to sign a contract with Lenin's government, received a cordial welcome back to Moscow. He signed a new contract to build a gigantic fertilizer complex in the Soviet Union, and to exchange $8 billion worth of chemical products over the next twenty years. As a token of the respect in which the Russians hold Hammer, his is one of the few private planes permitted to enter the USSR.

American firms bought licenses to use Russian inventions and technical processes. Reynolds Metals and Kaiser Aluminum acquired a Soviet method of pouring aluminum that raised productivity as much as 30 percent. The Russians bought licenses for the manufacture of American compressors, cash registers, pressurized plane doors, and other patents.

Exchanges of industrial scientists and engineers made it possible for each country's specialists to study the other's progress in power engineering, computer technology, electronics, laser techniques, polymers, and high-energy physics. A USSR–U.S. Joint Commission on Scientific and Technological Cooperation held its first session in Washington in March 1973. Russians and Americans undertook cooperative research in chemical catalysts, metallurgy, gas liquefication, coal mine dust control, and other industrial problems.

Over three hundred businessmen a week began flying to the Soviet Union. At a conference of the National Association of Manufacturers in Washington, Undersecretary of State William J. Casey was applauded when he declared that the old policy of hampering trade with the Russians was now obsolete.

Three American corporations combined to build a $10 billion pipeline to pump $45 billion worth of natural gas out of Siberia, to be liquefied and shipped in tankers to the United States. Planned to get gas flowing by 1980, the project was expected to provide up to 7 percent of U.S. consumption.

In preparation for this, and for laying a pipeline in Alaska to get the oil out of that icebound state, American permafrost specialists went to Yakutsk, Siberia, to study Soviet methods of construction in frozen subsoil. Russian permafrost specialists likewise visited Alaska to study American methods.

A new Soviet air route between Moscow and Washington was inaugurated in April 1974. Soon afterward a Pan Am subsidiary signed a contract to build the first American hotels in Moscow, Leningrad, and Kiev. American Express began opening travel offices throughout the Soviet Union.

Sen. Ted Stevens of Alaska, troubled by the inadequacy of training programs for American fishing fleets, visited the USSR to study the Leningrad Fishing Industry Sea School. His observations helped him write a new bill he introduced in Congress to improve U.S. maritime schooling. A Soviet training vessel for seamen, the sailing ship *Tovarisch*, visited U.S. maritime centers along the Atlantic seaboard.

Soviet-American exchanges were not limited to people and products. American striped perch and steelhead salmon were introduced into the Black Sea, where they adjusted well and thrived. American businessman J. Macbarron and farmer Joseph Givhan gave Soviet cattle breeders three pedigreed bull calves, to help the Altai Scientific Research Institute of Agriculture develop a long-haired, hardy breed of cattle for the Siberian climate.

California grape growers toured Soviet vineyards in the Crimea, exchanging useful shoptalk with their Russian equivalents. American arboretums and the Sochi experimental forest station in the Caucasus exchanged native trees for transplanting in each other's soil. Dr. Raymond Fosberg, Smithsonian botanist, was impressed with Soviet success in controlling insects through natural agents—other predatory insects, ants, and birds—without spraying.

American conservationists visited Soviet wild life preserves to study Russian methods of preserving beaver, elk, deer, wild boar, and bison in "survival centers." A joint Soviet-American working group was formed to cooperate in conserving rare and endangered species of animals and plant life.

A joint working group on water pollution met in Moscow. To study each other's purification techniques, Russian specialists went to Lake Tahoe, California, while U.S. specialists went to the Oka basin east of Moscow.

The Americans brought home a Soviet technique to study the Delaware and Ohio rivers. The Russians used an American plan for studying the Seversky Donets River.

A joint investigative group on air pollution selected Leningrad and St. Louis for combined study and comparison. After a working conference in Leningrad, Harvard meteorologist James R. Mahoney declared that the Soviet Union had "some of the best examples in the world" of planning for urban air pollution control, and that the Americans would be bringing home some of these plans for adaptation in the cities of the United States.

"We are now very confident that our program will

succeed in cleaning the atmosphere," said Dr. Herbert L. Wiser of the U.S. Environmental Protection Agency, "not only of St. Louis and of Leningrad, but of all big cities of the world."

American and Soviet scientists joined forces on an expedition in the Bering Sea to explore weather-shaping patterns for better long-range forecasting. A joint oceanographic force cooperated in deep-sea drilling to study submarine oil deposits, as well as in determining the best fish-breeding grounds. Soviet and American seismologists worked together at each other's research centers to develop better earthquake forecasting and warning systems.

In the field of medicine, American cancer and heart disease specialists spent up to a year at Soviet research centers, exchanging places with Russian specialists who came here.

U.S. News & World Report noted, "There have been some surprises for the American medical men, who have found that the Soviets are ahead in some aspects of heart and cancer research, in health protection for industrial workers, and in such fields as fast ambulance service and the use of paramedical personnel to speed emergency care for victims of accidents or sudden illness."

Soviet and American heart surgeons held a symposium on heart disease at the National Institutes of Health in Bethesda, Maryland. Prof. Vladimir Burakovsky, Director of the Institute of Cardiovascular Surgery, explained the value of such face-to-face contacts: "Comparing your own findings with information in published literature is one thing; getting direct personal assurance that my comrades and I are on the right track is another." U.S. heart specialist Dr. Frank Gerbode declared that it was enormously helpful, in turn, for Americans to be allowed to attend heart surgery by great Soviet specialists, who "have been responsible for some of the greatest achievements in this field."

In January 1973 a remarkable example of Soviet-American medical cooperation took place. Prof. Mstislav Keldyish, President of the Soviet Academy of Sciences, became gravely ill in Moscow, requiring complicated heart surgery of a kind in which Prof. Michael De Bakey of Houston was recognized as the world's greatest practitioner. When the Soviet Academy appealed to Dr. De Bakey, he flew at once to Moscow and cooperated in a three-and-one-half-hour successful operation.

To improve heart research, Soviet and American doctors are synchronizing an investigative procedure which will be used to examine ten thousand heart patients in each country.

In the fall of 1973 a Telex line was opened between the USSR Ministry of Health and the U.S. Department of Health, Education and Welfare, to facilitate cooperation in medical science and public health, with emphasis on heart disease, cancer, arthritis, and environmental health. Five Soviet anticancer drugs are presently being tested in the United States, which is also studying Russian methods of precancer examination and detection.

American specialists dealing with handicapped children were eager to compare notes in this field with the Russians. In 1974 they came from ten states to meet with Soviet researchers in the first U.S.–USSR Seminar on the Education of the Handicapped. "I was very much impressed by the education and the sincerity of the teacher in the classroom and the general happiness of the children," observed Dr. Jack Matthews, chairman of the Department of Speech, University of Pittsburgh.

Goodwill gestures marked the onset of a new joint space

program. During a tour of the Soviet Union, U.S. astronaut Scott Carpenter grafted an American shoot onto a Friendship tree planted in Sochi by Yuri Gagarin, the first man to orbit the earth in space. Scientists in Irkutsk who discovered a new mineral named it Armstrongite, after Neil Armstrong, the first man to set foot on the moon.

In July 1973 American astronauts and Soviet cosmonauts began preparing for flights of the Soyuz and Apollo spaceships which, in 1975, would rendezvous and dock, then orbit for forty-eight hours as a Soviet-American space station. The crew of the Soyuz went to Houston to study the design and procedures of the Apollo, and the crew of the Apollo went to the Cosmonaut Training Center in Stellar Town, USSR, to study the Soyuz.

In addition to studying each other's language, they learned a new technical space terminology both would speak. Return trips in 1974 and 1975 let the crews train together.

"The Soviet cosmonauts are a great bunch of guys," said U.S. astronaut Vance Brandt warmly. "We've come to know each other and get along very well. I have the greatest confidence that the joint flight will strengthen the friendship between the United States and the Soviet Union." U.S. astronaut Alan Bean declared, "When I get home, I'm going to tell my friends about my new impressions of Russia and the Russian people. I think it will change a good many concepts. This is a beautiful country, and I'm glad that we will be working together."

At the end of 1974 the Russians successfully tested docking procedures in trial orbits of the Soyuz with two cosmonauts aboard.

And in 1975 the three-man crew of the Apollo became the first Americans to visit the secret Soviet launching center in central Asia as they completed their joint training with

The Soyuz crew. In July the three Apollo astronauts rendezvoused in space with the two cosmonauts in the Soyuz. After docking, they exchanged visits and the first international handshake in space was witnessed on TV all over the world. The mission was hailed in both countries as a dramatic symbol of détente.

"This international project represents a long step forward," noted Soviet Academician Boris Petrov, "in the exploration and use of space for peaceful purposes." Eventually there will be joint voyages to other planets. The possibility of extraterrestrial civilizations is one that intrigues both Russian and American scientists and spacemen.

The U.S. Atomic Energy Commission and the USSR Committee for the Use of Atomic Energy are engaged in joint studies of safer and more efficient uses of nuclear energy for peaceful purposes. South of Moscow physicists of both countries are working together on experiments that use a powerful Soviet accelerator, and a U.S. computer for data processing.

★ ☆

Russians and Americans are also drawing together on the cultural front. When the New York City Ballet toured the USSR, over 100,000 Soviet ballet lovers jammed their twenty-eight sellout performances. The American dancers in turn lost no opportunity to attend the Russian ballet. "I think every dancer in America dreams of going to Russia," observed Gelsey Kirkland, "and as soon as I arrived, I loved it. . . . [Theirs is] about the most exciting dancing I have ever seen."

"It helps on every level possible—dancing, choreography, dance history, and the cultures of the two countries," declared American choreographer Jerome Robbins.

The tour was a homecoming for choreographer George Balanchine, born and trained in Leningrad. "A unique thing is happening now," he explained, "because when international relations improve, then the arts always flourish. We were all waiting for this so long, and I think now it will continue."

Seven years after his last concert, Van Cliburn returned to play for audiences in Moscow and Leningrad who applauded wildly and strewed the stage with flowers.

Duke Ellington and his band gave twenty-two concerts in five cities, where audiences demanded encores lasting well over an hour, then smothered him in flowers and embraces. At a jammed reception in Friendship House sponsored by the Institute of Soviet-American Relations, Ellington told his Russian admirers, "I feel very much at home in my tour of the Soviet Union. I feel I am not only among friends, I am among brothers, and I want you to know that any time you need a pianist at home, call me!"

American composers have become increasingly popular with Russians. The Leningrad Concert Orchestra has offered programs of Gershwin, Cole Porter, Leonard Bernstein, and Burt Bacharach. Soviet audiences have also enjoyed stage performances of *Our Town* and *Inherit the Wind* by the Arena Stage Theater of Washington, and a touring company of *Holiday On Ice*. Americans, in turn, were treated to tours of the Leningrad Philharmonic, Siberian and Armenian folk ensembles, and the world-famous Bolshoi Ballet.

The show business weekly, *Variety*, ran a banner headline on its August 7, 1974, front page: U.S.-SOVIET NEAR SHOW BIZ DETENTE. Tom Luddy, program director of the Pacific Film Archives in Berkeley, attended the Eighth Moscow International Film Festival to obtain Soviet documentaries for U.S. screenings.

"There's a well-traveled route now from New York to Moscow and from San Francisco to Vladivostok," he declared. "I'd like to cover this route with some films under my arm, and bring back films about life in Siberia."

CBS Records International signed a contract with the Soviet record company, Melodiya, for joint manufacture and distribution of each other's recording artists. *Literaturnaya Gazeta* revealed that in Moscow alone there are now five thousand rock groups, amateur and professional. The most popular group is a long-haired, blue-jeaned quartet, Blue Guitars.

Russian singer Muslim Magomayer, whose records have sold over 12 million copies in the USSR, brought down the house in Moscow recently when he switched from singing traditional concert numbers to an imitation of Louis Armstrong singing "When the Saints Go Marching In" in phonetic English, with rock body movements.

To show Americans the diversity of folk culture in fifteen different Soviet republics, the Soviet Ministry of Culture opened an arts and crafts exhibit in Washington. Attracting 100,000 visitors, it toured five American cities.

Armand Hammer arranged an art exchange with the Russians, getting the Hermitage and Pushkin museums to tour "Treasures of Soviet Museums," a rare collection of impressionist paintings, in the United States for the first time. His own collection was loaned to the Pushkin Museum in Moscow, and he donated a priceless Goya to the Hermitage in Leningrad.

Seattle, the port city whose IWW dockworkers once went on strike to help Lenin's revolution, became the first American city to adopt a "sister city" in the USSR—Tashkent. "We know that it has schools where the Russian language is taught," observed Vakhid Kazimov, Tashkent City Soviet chairman. "And we, in turn, have specialized English language schools. It is a pleasure to note that the schoolchildren of Tashkent and Seattle are already corresponding."

Student-teacher groups toured the Soviet Union in ever-increasing numbers. "I have fallen in love with Leningrad," declared Elmer Jackson of Fairbanks, Alaska. His group was welcomed by a large crowd of Soviet youth, with whom they held a seminar.

"We discussed everything under the sun," said Joseph Rem, "from dating habits to Vietnam, from women's rights to the history of the Soviet Union, from sex to the Middle East situation, the position of the UN and national minorities. . . . They know more about our country than we know about theirs."

Conference cochairman James Boldt was impressed by the Soviet system of finding jobs for everyone. "We can certainly take a good example from what the Soviets have done—and they have no unemployment." He added, "It's a more open society than most Americans think."

"Soviet people," said Alexander Gonzales of Los Angeles, "are not the devils I was taught they were at school."

When students and teachers from Syosset High School, Long Island, visited Moscow, biology teacher Jack Taylor was impressed with the "lively response, interest, and enthusiasm" of Russian students. Myra Kempler "loved the feeling of informality," admiring how well prepared students were for the day's lessons. Other American students had mixed feelings, some finding the classes too organized, with students standing up to answer questions. They also reacted unfavorably to Soviet school uniforms.

"Well," pointed out one Russian teen-ager, "the sweater and jeans most of you wear are a kind of uniform, too."

Delegations of Soviet young people visited American cities as guests of the American-Soviet Youth Forum, meeting with students, workers, and professionals under thirty.

There were also exchanges of gymnasts. The six top Soviet gymnasts, winners of the Munich Olympics, toured the United States as "The Six Graces." Their stunning performances captivated American audiences.

To raise money to send an American team of gymnasts to the Soviet Union, Russian trampolinists competed with American tumblers in five U.S. cities, using American equipment.

In July 1973 Soviet and American athletes held a track and field meet at the Dynamo Stadium in Minsk, before an audience of 65,000, the eleventh of a series. The Russians took first place in twenty-two events, the Americans in fourteen. Junior athletes competed at the same time in Odessa. Here Americans swept the track events, while the Russians excelled in the high jump and the javelin throw.

The following year an American team of nineteen mountain climbers successfully tackled 23,405-foot Lenin Peak in southeastern Russia. The Soviet Mountaineering Federation provided advisory and base-camp support, the first full-scale support between Soviet and American alpinists.

Détente brought a great upsurge in the exchange of Soviet and American literature. Today 435 American libraries, booksellers, and publishing houses receive over eight thousand copies of Soviet books annually, and approximately the same number of American books come to the Lenin Library in Moscow.

The USSR Library of Foreign Literature held an exhibit late in 1973 called "Books From the United States," many of them by American writers also published in the Soviet Union. Russian fans of Erskine Caldwell's novels packed the library auditorium to hear him speak. Calling for closer cultural relations, he declared, "It's what the world needs because we've been too far apart intellectually much too long."

Visiting the USSR as a guest of the Soviet Writers Union, American poet Reed Whittemore found some ambivalence among Russians about cultural exchanges. While they were deeply interested in the American scene, they seemed to him somewhat apprehensive about opening Russia to its ideas.

"Soviet defensiveness is hard for an American to understand," he reported, "because we think *we* have been defensively holding *them* off for three-quarters of a century. But it is obvious that they think *they* will not survive if they can't keep us out. . . . Not just our soldiers and shekels, but the whole capitalist 'sickness' is what they fear, from modernism to Coca-Cola."

In 1974 a historic publishing event occurred—the American publication of the first volumes of a thirty-volume edition of *The Great Soviet Encyclopedia*. The publisher said that the translation would mirror the Soviet culture for Americans as the Russians see themselves.

Although the cold war had given way to détente, a different kind of battle was fought between the United States and the USSR in September 1972. Over a chessboard American Bobby Fischer took the world championship away from Boris Spassky after twenty-four straight years of Russian victory. The contest won world attention when it was held in Reykjavik, Iceland, and televised to millions of chess fans all over the world.

Fischer's temperamental behavior did not win him many friends, either in the USSR or the United States, but it put a psychological strain on the Soviet grandmaster that helped Fischer win. The symbolism of the contest struck editorial writers of all nations. This kind of rivalry, and not a battlefield, they agreed, offered the proper channel for the keenly competitive spirit of both Russians and Americans. Fischer subsequently lost the championship, which reverted to the USSR when he refused to play a new Russian challenger unless the rules were changed as he demanded.

An official delegation of the United Automobile Workers toured the USSR's automobile plants. "We have no secrets," a Moscow Compact Car Plant executive told them. "Just let us know what you want to see." The auto workers were impressed by the company's housing for workers, thirteen kindergartens, vacation hotel in the Crimea, two Young Pioneer summer camps, clinic with 60 doctors and 106 nurses, technical school, stadium, and swimming pool—all paid for by profit sharing.

An official delegation of United Electrical, Radio, and Machine Workers who toured Soviet industrial plants were flabbergasted to discover that the Russian trade unions had the power to fire management executives who did a poor job.

By 1973, over ninety thousand American tourists a year were traveling to the Soviet Union. The Russians added a New York-to-Leningrad run to their air services, and Intourist expanded its operations to provide six thousand miles of car and bus itineraries.

Only some nine thousand Russians were able to visit the United States that year, but the number was increasing annually. One who came was Soviet historian Robert Ivanov, who went to Abilene, Kansas, to collect material for a Russian biography of Eisenhower. Prof. Maclyn Burg, head of the oral history division of the Eisenhower Library, invited Ivanov to be his guest. Burg, in turn, was invited to Moscow, where he lectured at the Institute of World History on the American concept of preserving the past in oral records.

Returning Nixon's visit to the Soviet Union, Leonid Brezhnev came to the United States in June 1974, to join in signing an impressive array of new bilateral agreements on all phases of Soviet-American relations. At a Blair House luncheon attended by the nation's business leaders, he expressed gratification that the cold war was finally over.

"I ask you, gentlemen, as I ask myself, was this a good period?" he said. "Did it serve the interest of the peoples? And my answer to that is no, no, no, and again no!"

In a TV address to Americans, he declared, "To live at peace, we must trust each other, and to trust one another, we must know each other better."

As he flew west with Nixon to San Clemente, they circled the Grand Canyon in Air Force One. Brezhnev revealed that he was a western film fan by mimicking a quick gun draw. Meeting western actor Chuck Connors at a twenty-six-hour Hollywood celebrity party in Nixon's California home, Brezhnev lifted him off his feet with an enthusiastic bear hug. Before the party was over Connors had won an agreement to coproduce a documentary with the Russian film industry. Connors described it as "strictly a capitalistic deal. We own 70 percent, and they get 30 percent."

The cigarette-smoking party chairman complained to a congressman from a tobacco state that his favorite brand of American cigarettes weren't as flavorsome as they had been. Spotting a familiar face among newsmen, he whooped, "I remember you from Moscow!" At Camp David he delighted photographers by driving an electric golf cart. The formal proceedings of signing an arms-limitation pact were lightened when he challenged the president to a race in signing their copies.

An agreement was reached for providing for joint U.S.–

USSR teams to undertake a new five-year oceanographic study to help weather forecasting, fishery conservation, and discovery of underseas mineral deposits. A new agricultural pact coordinated crop estimates, so that American farmers could anticipate Soviet needs. A new transportation pact arranged exchanges of information and personnel, and joint research in building highways, bridges, and tunnels, operating railroads in subzero weather, and cargo containerization.

A new six-year cultural pact increased the number of exchanges of graduate students, language teachers, performing groups, and artists. It also increased the circulation of *Amerika* and *Soviet Life* in each country. A Soviet–U.S. Chamber of Commerce was created to promote contacts between American businessmen and Russian trade officials.

Both governments pledged ten years of cooperation in studying peaceful uses of nuclear energy. A new tax agreement erased double taxation of citizens of one country who worked in the other. In a civil aviation pact, commercial air routes between the two countries were expanded cooperatively.

Perhaps the most important of the new treaties was an agreement to avoid military confrontations, both with each other and with each other's allies, and to consult immediately in case of a threat of nuclear war anywhere in the world.

One influential American senator, Henry Jackson, was not yet fully ready to make his own peace with the Russians. He put pressure on the Brezhnev mission to let more Soviet Jews emigrate to Israel, indicating that otherwise he would oppose ratification of the trade treaties. Jackson ignored the fact that the United States had already signed a May 1972 treaty pledging "noninterference in internal affairs" of the Soviet Union.

Senator Fulbright opposed Jackson's position. "It is simply not within the legitimate range of our foreign policy to instruct the Russians in how to treat their own people," he pointed out, "any more than it is Mr. Brezhnev's business to lecture us on our race relations or on such matters as the Indian protest at Wounded Knee. We would, quite properly, resent it, and so do they."

In departing, Brezhnev announced that Soviet-American détente was now "irreversible." The Politburo added a postscript upon his return to Moscow: "The Soviet people highly appreciate the fact that during Comrade L. I. Brezhnev's visit, wide circles of the American public expressed their friendly feelings toward our people, and showed understanding of the importance of further developing Soviet-American relations."

There was some discord in the harmony, however, A faction of Russian Jews continued appealing to Americans to support their complaint that they were not being allowed to emigrate to Israel in sufficient numbers. A faction of Russian intellectuals also appealed to Americans to pressure the Kremlin into giving them the freedom to dissent. The leading figure in their movement was novelist Aleksandr Solzhenitsyn, who was forced into exile in Switzerland.

American Zionists strongly supported Senator Jackson's demands on behalf of the Russian Jews. American intellectuals were split on the Solzhenitsyn issue, some supporting him fully, others feeling that gradual liberalization of Soviet restrictions was more likely to come about through détente, and the growing exchange of people and information.

But many Russian intellectuals felt that détente would not help them win greater liberty to dissent. Physicist Andrei Sakharov, a Nobel Prize winner like Solzhenitsyn, declared, "The authorities . . . feel that with détente they can now ignore Western public opinion, which isn't going to be concerned with the plight of internal freedoms in Russia." Many American intellectuals managed to visit Sakharov during visits to the Soviet Union in a show of support.

When U.S. physicists attended the International Conference on Magnetism in Moscow in August 1973, they were upset upon learning that seven leading Jewish scientists had been barred from the session, allegedly for having applied for emigration visas to Israel. The seven had gone on a hunger strike to dramatize their grievance. After visiting them, the American physicists protested their exclusion.

Conference chairman Vonsofsky replied that they had been barred as "troublemakers," and that their papers would not be read because they had been submitted too late. Pointing out that Soviet law prohibited discrimination against Jews, he added that he himself had a Jewish wife, and so was even more unlikely to violate the law. Some American scientists felt that it was wrong to inject political questions into a scientific conference. Others considered the matter a purely internal problem for the Soviet government.

Thousands of American intellectuals and theater people signed a petition to the Soviet Union asking that Jewish ballet star Valery Panov and his non-Jewish wife and dancing partner, Galina Ragozina, be allowed to emigrate to Israel. Soon afterward the Panovs were granted exit visas, and in 1975 danced together in America before delighted ballet audiences.

Moscow charged that Zionist propaganda was principally responsible for giving Americans the impression that Jews as a class were discriminated against in the Soviet

Union. The government published scores of letters from Jewish emigrants who, disillusioned by their experience in Israel, were begging to be allowed to return home.

In December 1974 New York's TV Channel 5 reported that at least half of Israel's Russian emigrés had left.

When Senator Jackson succeeded in holding up ratification of the Soviet-American trade agreements, a Soviet spokesman asked in exasperation, "Should trade depend on our insistence that you solve your racial problems?"

"It is no accident," said Prof. Georgi Arbatov of the Soviet Institute for the Study of the United States, "that Senator Jackson, who is connected with the military-industrial companies, was so active in opposing ratification. . . . This same Senator, . . . as the *Washington Post* put it, is one of the leading cold-war exponents in Congress. . . . Most-favored-nation status is as much an interest to the American business community as it is a concern for us. If we don't have it—we will simply change suppliers."

★ ☆

In May 1974 a delegation of the Supreme Soviet visited the United States for the first time, receiving a warm welcome. Arrangements were made for future regular contacts between the Soviet and Congress to further détente.

The chief source of tension and anxiety between the two countries was the Middle East, where the United States was giving military aid to its client state, Israel, while the Soviet Union was following suit with its client state, Syria. Both superpowers, however, were careful to avoid getting involved with combat forces themselves. And each agreed to urge restraint on the hawks in its sphere of influence.

A major problem for the Russians arose in the summer of 1974 over President Nixon's troubles with Watergate. What would happen to détente if he were impeached or forced to resign? Worried, the Russians took pains to make it clear that they considered their new treaties to be with the American government, not just with any president. But Nixon tried to give Americans the impression that a continuation of détente depended upon his personal relationship with Brezhnev.

He arranged another summit with Brezhnev in Moscow in July. The two heads of state signed a few new agreements providing for further cooperation in housing, heart research, and energy problems, but the Russians were reluctant to enter into negotiations on disarmament with a president who had clearly lost his influence with Congress to get such an important treaty ratified.

With Nixon's forced resignation in August, President Gerald Ford sought to assure the Russians of a continuity of détente by keeping Kissinger on as secretary of state.

As a goodwill gesture, the Russians privately offered some concessions on their emigration policy, although they angrily denied it when Senator Jackson announced it publicly. Jackson nevertheless professed himself satisfied, and the Senate ratified all Soviet-American treaties, tying the emigration of Soviet Jewry to American granting of most-favored-nation trading status to the Russians.

"These days," *Newsweek* noted in December 1974, "formal signings of trade protocols—replete with TV cameras and bear hugs—are virtually weekly events in a frescoed room at the Foreign Trade Ministry. . . . Free-flowing vodka is as much a part of these occasions as polite Soviet inquiries about the wife and kids. . . . Already seventeen U.S. firms rent office space in Moscow. And the number of businessmen trekking to Russia is increasing so fast that a $110 million U.S.-sponsored trade center is now a-building on the banks of the Moskva."

The importance of this soaring trade to the United States was indicated by the fact that the Russians bought ten times as much as they sold to the Americans. Taking U.S. foodstuffs, machinery, and chemicals, they supplied raw materials, oil and oil products, diamonds, and furs. Over a hundred American firms received $385 million in orders for a single project—the world's largest truck plant being built at the Kama River.

In one month International Harvester sold the Russians $100 million worth of crawler tractors. Robert McMenamin, who negotiated the deal for the company, declared jubilantly, "The order represents two thousand man-years of work for us."

In the light of détente, most Americans today recognize that we probably misread Soviet intentions throughout the cold war. The Russians, far from planning military aggression against the West, had been so devastated by their terrible losses during the Second World War that they were determined to build defenses so strong that they could never again be successfully attacked and their land laid waste.

"We have been wrong on just about every major development in the USSR since the Bolshevik revolution," pointed out Fred Warner Neal, who had organized the Voice of America propaganda broadcasts to the Soviet Union. "We didn't anticipate the revolution; when it occurred, we didn't think it would succeed; when it was successful, we thought socialism was going to be abandoned; when it wasn't, we thought we wouldn't have to recognize the new Soviet state; when we did, we acted first as if it was like the Western democracies and then as if it was like the Nazis; when the Germans invaded, we thought the Russians could last only six weeks; when they survived the war, we thought they couldn't recover quickly from it; when they recovered quickly, we thought they didn't have the know-how to build missiles, and so on. This record would seem to suggest . . . that perhaps we should not be too positive in other assumptions we have made."

Joseph Stalin had also made frequent miscalculations about the United States. He had been confident that the depression of the early thirties would bring about revolution and the downfall of capitalism; it didn't. He had signed a pact with Hitler, believing that the United States was part of a Western plot to goad the Nazis into destroying the USSR, and that the Americans would never oppose fascism for that reason.

Wrong on both counts, after the war he saw American opposition to his policies in East Europe as proof of the determination of Washington to turn the cold war into a hot war. Stalin's judgment again proved faulty.

During the cold war leaders on both sides had exaggerated the dangers posed by each other. "President Kennedy alleged there was a missile gap," pointed out Senator Fulbright. "There was a missile gap but it was in reverse. We had about one thousand weapons and they had about eighty, whereas he made the country believe that we had eighty and they had a thousand. It just was not so. But the public believes that we are behind."

Fulbright pointed out further, "To attribute everything that goes wrong, or wrong from our point of view, to the Russians I think is unrealistic and not true. . . . The Middle East grew out of a conflict that had its origins long ago and that was not Russian-inspired."

Misunderstanding of Soviet motives had led George Kennan to draw up the first blueprints of American policy that developed into the cold war. Much later Kennan grew to realize, and publicly acknowledged, that the Soviet government had never intended to settle the historic dispute between socialism and capitalism by armed force. He attributed American misconceptions to a failure to understand Russian fears.

"The United States, let us remember," pointed out journalist John Gunther, "had been invaded only once in its entire history, during the War of 1812, and then with little damage. But look at Russia and its exposed and vulnerable western frontier! Russia has been invaded from the west fourteen different times in 150 years, and one city, Minsk, has been under foreign occupation 101 times since its foundation. True, the Russians have always managed to get rid of the invaders. This, however, took time, lives, and effort, and the Soviet Union doesn't want to have to go through the painful and laborious process ever again."

Armand Hammer, as capitalistic a businessman as our nation has ever produced, reminds us that the Soviet system has features which we can study with profit. "Maybe it's not as efficient as ours," he points out, "but it has other things going for it. There is no unemployment in Russia; everybody has a job. There is apparently plenty to eat, the people are well fed. . . . I didn't see any beggars in the street, I didn't see any people in rags. You see no signs of the extremes of poverty and wealth that we have in the Western world."

As for crime, ninety-seven lawyers of the District of Columbia bar who toured the USSR in 1973 found that three out of every four cases in court are civil, not criminal, cases. Most sentences, since Stalin, do not involve imprisonment. Penalties are fines, suspended sentences on probation, public censure, loss of rights to hold office for a period of time, and corrective labor, with the convicted person accompanied by his family when he is not permitted to continue working at his regular job.

Détente is not based solely on trust of the American and Russian governments in each other's good intentions. Such intentions are likely to remain good only so long as they serve each nation's own interests. Détente became possible when both superpowers recognized that they have very important interests in common, and that it would be to their mutual advantage to pursue them in a cooperative partnership.

This was so when Russians and Americans first became friends in our prerevolutionary days. It holds just as true in the world of today and tomorrow.

★ ☆

The SALT talks have started both nations down the road to eventual nuclear disarmament. The Stockholm International Peace Research Institute points out that the United States and the USSR have stockpiled between them an explosive force equal to fifteen tons of TNT for every man, woman, and child on earth. UNESCO points out that more is spent each year on armaments than on public health and education.

In December 1974 President Gerald Ford flew to Vladivostok to meet Brezhnev. They reached a new arms limitation agreement setting a nuclear arms ceiling for both nations.

Kissinger called the Vladivostok agreement "putting a cap on the arms race," but Senator Jackson led critics who protested that the weapons ceilings had been set too high.

Détente suffered a setback in January 1975 when the Soviet Union decided it could not ratify the new favored-nation trade treaty because of Jackson's clause making it contingent upon Moscow's acceptance of American dictation of Soviet policy on Jewish emmigration. The treaty was not denounced or repudiated but merely set aside until Congress withdrew the Jackson amendment.

The continued success of détente will depend in some measure on the caliber of the Americans we send to Moscow

The continued success of deténte will depend in some measure on the caliber of the Americans we send to Moscow to represent us and keep us informed. "A vain, fussy, and ignorant ambassador," warns George Kennan, "is capable of . . . doing lasting . . . damage to the fabric of Russian-American relations." A Moscow correspondent, Herbert Matthews of the *New York Times* notes, should "feel sympathy and liking for the Russian people however anti-Communist he might be."

Realists, the Russians do not expect that all Soviet-American differences are now going to disappear magically.

Leonid Brezhnev told the American people during his visit to the United States, "Much has already been accomplished in the development of Soviet-American relations. But we are still standing at the very beginning of a long road. We must show constant concern to protect and nurture the fresh shoots of good relations."

Lev Tolkunov, editor in chief of *Izvestia*, declares, "It will take time and infinite patience to create and adjust something which has never existed before—the machinery of cooperation."

CHRONOLOGY OF EVENTS
IN U.S.-SOVIET HISTORY

1741	Bering expedition to Alaska.
1745-1764	Trading posts open in Russian America.
1780	Continental Congress sends Dana as envoy to Catherine the Great.
1788	John Paul Jones fights under Russian flag.
1796	Russian American Company chartered.
1804	Jefferson and Tsar Alexander I correspond.
1809	John Quincy Adams first U.S. Minister to Russia. Tsar aids U.S. shipping against France.
1811	Russians open trading post in California.
1819	Astor fur traders' corruption of Indians leads to U.S. trader ban in Russian America.
1823	Monroe Doctrine puts tsar's Holy Alliance on notice to keep out of the Americas.
1825	Decembrists draft U.S.-style constitution and seek to overthrow Tsar Nicholas I.
1832	Buchanan negotiates U.S.-Russian trade treaty.
1841	Russian American Company leaves California.
1848	Tsar's intervention in Hungary creates antitsarist sentiment in United States.
1853	Americans support Russia in Crimean War.
1856	Turgenev supports American abolitionists.
1861	Tsar Alexander II frees Russian serfs.

1863   Lincoln issues Emancipation Proclamation. Russian fleet winters in American ports.

1867   Seward buys Alaska from the Russians.

1868   Mark Twain visits Russia.

1883–1910   **Large-scale immigration of Russian Jews fleeing tsarist pogroms.**

1891–1892   Americans send famine aid to Russia.

1900   Americans and Russians allies in Boxer Rebellion.

1903   Americans protest Kishinev pogrom.

1904   Kennan agitates against Tsar Nicholas II among Russian troops imprisoned in Japan.

1905   **Kennan's agitation helps spur 1905 Revolution. T. Roosevelt arbitrates Russo-Japanese War.**

1905–1907   **Isadora Duncan dances and teaches in Russia.**

1911   Congress abrogates trade treaty of 1832 because tsar refuses to recognize U.S. naturalization of Russian Jewish refugees.

1914   House of Morgan floats war loan to tsar.

1916   American-Russian Chamber of Commerce formed to protect U.S. investments and trade in Russia.

1917   Trotsky in exile in New York City. Wilson supports Kerensky Revolution. America enters World War I, becoming Russian ally. Root mission tries to hold Russians in war. Robins heads American Red Cross relief to Russian war famine victims. Wilson opposes Bolshevik revolution. Bolsheviks brand World War I an imperialist struggle. Seattle seamen support Lenin.

1918   Wilson's Fourteen Points speech answers Bolsheviks. Russian-German Brest-Litovsk peace treaty chills Soviet-American relations. Wilson spurns Trotsky offer to keep Russia in war if swift U.S. aid reaches Soviets. Lenin writes "Letter to American Workers," inspiring "Hands off Russia" movement. American Communist party formed.

1918–1920   American troop intervention in Siberia.

1919   State Department refuses to recognize credentials of first Soviet representative to U.S.

1920 U.S. deports Russian "undesirables." John Reed dies; buried with honors in Moscow. Harding lifts economic blockade against Soviets to help U.S. postwar slump.

1921 U.S. businessmen view Lenin's New Economic Policy as return to capitalism. Armand Hammer negotiates trade deals with Lenin. First Ford tractors arrive in Soviet Union.

1921-1923 Hoover famine aid to Russians. Spargo plan to use food as weapon to overturn Bolsheviks. Friends of Soviet Russia mount separate aid program.

1922 Hillman modernizes Soviet clothing industry.

1924 Lenin's death gets hostile U.S. press notices. Amtorg Trading Corp. opens in New York City.

1925 American engineers begin working in USSR.

1926-1927 U.S. businessmen reassured by Stalin ouster of Trotsky; see USSR put on "a business basis." American tourists begin trips through Russia. Cultural exchanges begin.

1928 Stalin utilizes American engineers in his Five-Year Plan to industrialize USSR.

1931 U.S. clergy find USSR a moral society. Hoover calls for its destruction. Over 100,000 U.S. workers apply for 12,000 Soviet jobs.

1933 Roosevelt recognizes Soviet government.

1934 U.S. journey by Russian satirists Ilf and Petrov results in book *Little Golden America*.

1935 AFL rejects Soviet offer to form international united labor front against fascism.

1936 Americans fight with Soviet aid in Spain against Franco-Hitler-Mussolini forces.

1937 U.S. Ambassador Davies attends Moscow trials. Stalin introduces new Soviet constitution, calling it more liberal than U.S. constitution.

1939 Stalin's nonaggression pact with Hitler causes split in U.S. anti-Fascist movement.

1940 FDR warns Stalin of planned Hitler double cross.

Chronology of Events in U.S.-Soviet History

1941   When Nazis invade USSR, FDR pledges U.S. aid to Russians. American isolationists predict quick collapse of the Soviets. Stalin invites U.S. troops on Soviet soil as allies. Lend-Lease supplies go to USSR in North Sea convoys. Pearl Harbor makes U.S. and USSR full war allies.

1942   Russians press U.S. for second front.

1943   Battle of Stalingrad wins great American admiration. Lack of second front leads to Teheran Conference. FDR and Stalin draw closer.

1944   Second front creates pro-American enthusiasm in USSR.

1945   At Yalta Conference FDR makes concessions to Stalin, and Stalin pledges to join war against Japan. U.S.-Soviet relations chill after FDR's death as Truman takes a hard line. U.S. and Soviet forces link up at the Elbe, and Germans soon surrender. Eisenhower lionized in Moscow visit. At Potsdam Conference Truman and Stalin clash over postwar organization of East Europe. Russian attack in Manchuria and U.S. atom bombs on Hiroshima and Nagasaki force Japan's surrender.

1946   Cold war begins. Truman rejects Soviet disarmament proposals. Stalin keeps control of East Europe. Truman encircles USSR with air bases. V.P. Wallace protests, is forced to resign.

1947   Truman Doctrine and Marshall Plan prop up shaky Western governments. Stalin revives Comintern.

1948   Berlin blockade and American airlift.

1949   Acheson organizes NATO. USSR explodes own atom bomb.

1950   Korean War begins.

1951   Congress abrogates U.S.-USSR trade agreement.

1952   Moscow accuses U.S. of germ warfare in Korea. U.S. bans American travel to USSR and East Europe.

1953   Stalin dies. Eisenhower works out Korean truce with Russians. U.S. executes Rosenbergs as Soviet spies.

1954   Dulles threatens "massive retaliation" against USSR to deter revolutions.

1955   Geneva Conference. Eisenhower presents "open skies" proposal for disarmament treaty to Khrushchev. Cordial "spirit of Geneva" leads to beginning of cultural, scientific, and trade exchanges.

1956   Khrushchev announces new "coexistence policy." Hungarian revolt holds up progress.

1957   USSR launches Sputnik, leading U.S. to begin crash program to catch up in space science.

1958   U.S.-USSR agreement to cooperate in cultural, educational, technical, and sports fields. U.S. launches space satellite Explorer.

1959   U.S. and USSR exchange scientific technology and expeditions. Nixon and Khrushchev clash in Moscow "kitchen debate." Khrushchev visits U.S. A new cordial "spirit of Camp David."

1960   Paris Conference wrecked when American U-2 spy plane shot down by Soviets over Russia. Khrushchev denounces U.S. at UN.

1961   Cosmonaut Gagarin orbits earth. Kennedy begins racing Russians to the moon. Bay of Pigs invasion turns Cuba toward Russians. Kennedy and Khrushchev clash in Vienna. Communists in East Germany build Berlin Wall.

1962   World fears nuclear war over Cuban missile crisis. Khrushchev-Kennedy compromise saves peace.

1963   Nuclear test ban treaty ends atomic fallout.

1965   Johnson escalation of Vietnam War slows improvement in U.S.-USSR relations. American bombers hit Hanoi during Kosygin visit.

1966   Johnson lifts anti-Soviet trade ban. U.S.-USSR treaty on exploration of outer space.

1967   Johnson-Kosygin summit conference at Glassboro. They consult during Middle East six-day war over direct "hot line." Air services begin between New York and Moscow.

1968   U.S.-USSR nonproliferation treaty checks spread of nuclear weapons. Soviet suppression of Czech uprising halts further U.S.-USSR negotiations.

Chronology of Events in U.S.-Soviet History

1969   SALT talks begin to curb nuclear arms race.

1971   U.S. and USSR coordinate space programs.

1972   Détente ends cold war. Nixon and Brezhnev sign wide-ranging agreements in Moscow creating U.S.-Soviet cooperation in every area of trade, education, the arts, and sciences. Trade triples.

1973   Joint U.S.-Soviet commissions begin cooperative research, exchanging specialists in all fields. Over 90,000 American tourists visit USSR.

1974   Visiting U.S., Brezhnev signs more U.S.-Soviet treaties of cooperation. Still more signed when Nixon returns the visit. Nixon's downfall does not affect détente. Ford meets Brezhnev in Vladivostok and negotiates arms limitation agreement. Friction develops over Soviet policy on Jewish emigration to Israel.

1975   *Apollo-Soyuz* space flight dramatizes détente.

BIBLIOGRAPHY
AND
RECOMMENDED READING

Adams, Sherman. *First-Hand Report*. New York: Harper & Row, 1961.

Allen, Frederick Lewis. *Only Yesterday*. New York: Bantam Books, 1946.

Angle, Paul M., ed. *The Uneasy World*. Greenwich, Conn.: Fawcett Publications, 1968.

*Archer, Jules. *Chou En-lai*. New York: Hawthorn Books, 1973.

*_____. *The Dictators*. New York: Hawthorn Books, 1967.

*_____. *Man of Steel: Joseph Stalin*. New York: Julian Messner, 1965.

*_____. *Mao Tse-tung*. New York: Hawthorn Books, 1972.

*_____. *Resistance*. Philadelphia: Macrae Smith Co., 1973.

_____. *Strikes, Bombs & Bullets*. New York: Julian Messner, 1972.

_____. *Thorn in Our Flesh: Castro's Cuba*. New York: Cowles Book Co., 1970.

*_____. *Trotsky: World Revolutionary*. New York: Julian Messner, 1973.

_____. *World Citizen: Woodrow Wilson*. New York: Julian Messner, 1967.

*Appel, Benjamin. *With Many Voices*. New York: William Morrow & Co., 1963.

*Barghoorn, Frederick C. *The Soviet Image of the United States*. New York: Harcourt, Brace & Co., 1950.

*Barnet, Richard J. *Intervention and Revolution*. New York and Cleveland: The World Publishing Co., 1968.

*recommended reading

Bibliography and Recommended Reading

Baruch, Bernard M. *Baruch: The Public Years*. New York: Holt, Rinehart & Winston, 1960.

Berky, Andrew S., and Shenton, James P. *The Historians' History of the United States*. New York: G. P. Putnam's Sons, 1966.

*Bohlen, Charles E. *The Transformation of American Foreign Policy*. New York: W. W. Norton & Co., 1969.

Bowers, Claude G. *The Young Jefferson*. Boston: Houghton Mifflin Co., 1969.

Bowles, Chester. *Promises to Keep*. New York: Harper & Row, 1971.

*Bradley, John. *Allied Intervention in Russia*. New York: Basic Books, 1968.

Brower, Brock. *Other Loyalties*. New York: Atheneum, 1968.

*Carr, Albert Z. *Truman, Stalin and Peace*. Garden City, N.Y.: Doubleday & Co., 1950.

*Chevigny, Hector. *Russian America*. New York: Viking Press, 1965.

Christian, George. *The President Steps Down*. New York: The Macmillan Co., 1970.

Coffin, Tristram. *Senator Fulbright*. New York: E. P. Dutton & Co., 1966.

Commager, Henry Steele. *Freedom and Order*. Cleveland and New York: The World Publishing Co., 1966.

Committee on Un-American Activities, House of Representatives. *Guerrilla Warfare Advocates in the United States*. Washington, D.C.: U.S. Government Printing Office, 1968.

Constitution of the Union of Soviet Socialist Republics. Moscow: Foreign Languages Publishing House, 1962.

*Crankshaw, Edward. *Khrushchev Remembers*. Boston and Toronto: Little, Brown & Co., 1970.

*Davies, Joseph E. *Mission to Moscow*. New York: Simon & Schuster, 1941.

Day, Donald, ed. *Woodrow Wilson's Own Story*. Boston: Little, Brown & Co., 1952.

De Launay, Jacques. *Secret Diplomacy of World War II*. New York: Simmons-Boardman, 1963.

Dennett, Tyler. *Roosevelt and the Russo-Japanese War*. Garden City, N.Y.: Doubleday, Page & Co., 1925.

*Deutscher, Isaac. *The Great Contest: Russia and the West*. New York and London: Oxford University Press, 1960.

_____. *Stalin: A Political Biography*. New York: Vintage Books, 1962.

Djilas, Milovan. *Conversations with Stalin*. New York: Harcourt, Brace & World, 1962.

Donnelly, Desmond. *Struggle for the World*. New York: St. Martin's Press, 1965.

*Douglas, William O. *Russian Journey*. Garden City, N.Y.: Doubleday & Co., 1956.

Duranty, Walter. *I Write as I Please*. New York: Halcyon House, 1935.

Eisenhower, Dwight D. *Crusade in Europe*. Garden City, N.Y.: Doubleday & Co., 1948.

_____. *Waging Peace*. Garden City, N.Y.: Doubleday & Co., 1965.

_____. *Mandate for Change*. New York: New American Library, 1965.

*Filene, Peter G. *Americans and the Soviet Experiment*. Cambridge, Mass.: Harvard University Press, 1967.

Fischer, Louis. *The Life of Lenin*. New York, Evanston, and London: Harper & Row, 1964.

Gellhorn, Martha. *The Face of War*. New York: Simon & Schuster, 1959.

Geyelin, Philip. *Lyndon B. Johnson and the World*. New York, Washington, and London: Frederick A. Praeger, 1966.

Goldman, Eric F. *The Tragedy of Lyndon Johnson*. London: Macdonald & Co., 1969.

Goldwater, Barry M. *Why Not Victory?* New York: Macfadden-Bartell Corp., 1963.

Greenfield, Kent Roberts, ed. *Command Decisions*. New York: Harcourt, Brace & Co., 1959.

Grodzins, Morton, and Rabinowitch, Eugene, eds. *The Atomic Age*. New York and London: Basic Books, 1963.

*Gromyko, Anatoli, and Shvedkov, Yuri. *USSR–USA Relations Today*. Moscow: Novosti Press Agency Publishing House, 1973.

Gunther, John. *Eisenhower*. New York: Harper & Brothers, 1952.

*_____. *Inside Russia Today*. New York: Harper & Brothers, 1958.

_____. *Procession*. New York, Evanston, and London: Harper & Row, 1965.

Bibliography and Recommended Reading

Hassett, William D. *Off the Record with F.D.R.* London: George Allen & Unwin, 1960.

Hayter, William. *Russia and the World.* New York: Taplinger Publishing Co., 1970.

*Hicks, Granville. *One of Us: The Story of John Reed.* New York: Equinox Press, 1935.

Hohenberg, John. *New Era in the Pacific.* New York: Simon & Schuster, 1972.

*Horowitz, David. *The Free World Colossus.* New York: Hill & Wang, 1965.

Hindus, Maurice. *Crisis in the Kremlin.* Garden City, N.Y.: Doubleday & Co., 1953.

Hughes, Emmet John. *The Ordeal of Power.* New York: Atheneum, 1963.

*Ivanyan, E., and Kunina, A. *USSR–US Relations 1917–1973.* Moscow: Novosti Press Agency Publishing House, 1974.

Jacker, Corinne. *The Black Flag of Anarchy.* New York: Charles Scribner's Sons, 1968.

Jensen, Joan M. *The Price of Vigilance.* Chicago, New York, and San Francisco: Rand McNally & Co., 1968.

Johnson, Lyndon Baines. *The Vantage Point.* New York: Popular Library, 1971.

*Jones, Mervyn. *The Antagonists.* New York: Clarkson N. Potter, 1962.

*Kashlev, Y. *Cultural Contacts Promote Peaceful Coexistence.* Moscow: Novosti Press Agency Publishing House, 1974.

Kedward, Roderick. *The Anarchists.* New York: American Heritage Press, 1971.

*Kennan, George F. *American Diplomacy 1900–1950.* New York: New American Library, 1951.

*_____. *Memoirs 1925–1950.* Boston and Toronto: Little, Brown & Co., 1967.

*_____. *Russia and the West Under Lenin and Stalin.* Boston and Toronto: Little, Brown & Co., 1961.

Kennedy, John F. *A Nation of Immigrants.* New York and Evanston: Harper & Row, 1964.

Krock, Arthur. *In the Nation: 1932–1966.* New York, Toronto, London, and Sydney: McGraw-Hill Book Co., 1966.

Lasch, Christopher. *The New Radicalism in America.* New York: Vintage Books, 1965.

*Laserson, Max M. *The American Impact on Russia: 1784–1917.* New York: Collier Books, 1962.

*Lauterbach, Richard. *These Are the Russians.* New York: Book Find Club, 1945.

LaFeber, Walter. *The New Empire.* Ithaca, N.Y.: Cornell University Press, 1963.

Leish, Kenneth W., ed. *The American Heritage Pictorial History of the Presidents of the United States.* New York: American Heritage Publishing Co., 1968.

*Lenin, V. I. *Letter to American Workers.* Moscow: Novosti Press Agency Publishing House, 1973.

*Lens, Sidney. *The Futile Crusade.* Chicago: Quadrangle Books, 1964.

Leuchtenburg, William E. *Franklin D. Roosevelt and the New Deal.* New York: Harper & Row, 1963.

Lippmann, Walter. *Early Writings.* New York: Liveright, 1970.

_____. *Conversations with Walter Lippmann.* Boston and Toronto: Little, Brown & Co., 1965.

*Long, David F. *The Outward View.* Chicago, New York, and San Francisco: Rand McNally & Co., 1963.

Loth, David. *Swope of G.E.* New York: Simon & Schuster, 1958.

Madison, Charles A. *Leaders and Liberals in 20th Century America.* New York: Frederick Ungar Publishing Co., 1961.

*Mason, Daniel, and Smith, Jessica, eds. *Lenin's Impact on the United States.* New York: NWR Publications, 1970.

Matthews, Herbert L. *A World in Revolution.* New York: Charles Scribner's Sons, 1971.

Mazo, Earl. *Richard Nixon.* New York: Avon Books, 1960.

Meyer, Karl E., ed. *Senator Fulbright.* New York: Macfadden Books, 1964.

Mitgang, Herbert. *America at Random.* New York: Coward-McCann, 1969.

Moore, John Bassett. *The Works of James Buchanan,* vol. 2. Philadelphia and London: J. B. Lippincott Co., 1908.

Morgan, E. Delmar, and Coote, C. H. *Early Voyages to Russia and Persia.* London: The Hakluyt Society, 1886.

Morison, Samuel Eliot. *The Oxford History of the American People.* New York: Oxford University Press, 1965.

Morris, Richard B., ed. *Great Presidential Decisions.* Greenwich, Conn.: Fawcett Publications, 1960.

*Neal, Fred Warner. *U.S. Foreign Policy and the Soviet Union.* Santa Barbara, Calif.: Center for the Study of Democratic Institutions, 1961.

Padover, Saul K. *Jefferson.* New York: New American Library, 1964.

*Parenti, Michael. *The Anti-Communist Impulse.* New York: Random House, 1969.

Payne, Robert, ed. *The Civil War in Spain.* Greenwich, Conn.: Fawcett Publications, 1962.

Pethybridge, R. W. *A History of Postwar Russia.* New York: New American Library, 1966.

*Pierce, Richard A. *Russia's Hawaiian Adventure.* Berkeley and Los Angeles: University of California Press, 1965.

Pietromarchi, Luca. *The Soviet World.* London: George Allen & Unwin, 1965.

Pringle, Henry F. *Theodore Roosevelt.* New York: Harcourt, Brace & World, 1956.

Pullen, John J. *Patriotism in America.* New York: American Heritage Press, 1971.

*Radoshi, Ronald. *American Labor and United States Foreign Policy.* New York: Random House, 1969.

Reedy, George E. *The Twilight of the Presidency.* New York and Cleveland: World Publishing Co., 1970.

*Reeve, F. D. *Robert Frost in Russia.* Boston and Toronto: Little, Brown & Co., 1963.

Rollins, Alfred B., Jr. *Woodrow Wilson and the New America.* New York: Dell Publishing Co., 1965.

Rosner, Joseph. *The Hater's Handbook.* New York: Dell Publishing Co., 1965.

Ross, Ishbel. *Charmers & Cranks.* New York, Evanston, and London: Harper & Row, 1965.

*Russell, Bertrand. *Unarmed Victory.* New York: Simon & Schuster, 1963.

Ryabov, Vasili. *The Road of Valour and Glory*. Moscow: Novosti Press Agency Publishing House, undated.

Salisbury, Harrison E. *War Between Russia and China*. Toronto, New York, and London: Bantam Books, 1970.

Scheer, George F., and Rankin, Hugh F. *Rebels and Redcoats*. New York: New American Library, 1959.

Schlesinger, Arthur M., Jr. *A Thousand Days*. Boston: Houghton Mifflin Co., 1965.

Schuman, Frederick L. *The Cold War*. Baton Rouge, La.: Louisiana State University Press, 1962.

Seldes, George. *Freedom of the Press*. Indianapolis and New York: The Bobbs-Merrill Co., 1935.

_____. *You Can't Print That!* Garden City, N.Y.: Garden City Publishing Co., 1929.

Sherrill, Robert. *The Accidental President*. New York: Pyramid Books, 1968.

Shub, Anatole. *An Empire Loses Hope*. New York: W. W. Norton & Co., 1970.

Sinkler, George. *The Racial Attitudes of American Presidents*. Garden City, N.Y.: Doubleday & Co., 1971.

Sorenson, Charles E. *My Forty Years with Ford*. New York and London: Collier Books, 1956.

Spock, Benjamin. *Decent and Indecent*. New York: McCall Publishing Co., 1970.

*Starushenko, G. B., Golden, L. O., and Kotov, M. I., eds. *William Du Bois: Scholar, Humanitarian, Freedom Fighter*. Moscow: Novosti Press Agency Publishing House, 1971.

Stebbins, Richard P. *The United States in World Affairs 1966*. New York: Harper & Row, 1967.

Steel, Ronald. *Pax Americana*. New York: Viking Press, 1968.

Steffens, Lincoln. *Autobiography*. New York: Harcourt, Brace & World, 1958.

*Strakhousky, Leonid I. *American Opinion About Russia 1917–1920*. Toronto: University of Toronto Press, 1961.

Sulzberger, C. L. *A Long Row of Candles*. New York: The Macmillan Company, 1969.

Swing, Raymond. *"Good Evening!"* New York: Harcourt, Brace & World, 1964.

Syrett, Harold C., ed. *American Historical Documents*. New York: Barnes & Noble, 1960.

Teller, Judd L. *Strangers and Natives*. New York: Delacorte Press, 1968.

*Thayer, Charles W., and the editors of *Life*. *Russia*. New York: Time Incorporated, 1963.

Thayer, George. *The Farther Shores of Politics*. New York: Simon & Schuster, 1968.

Thornton, Willis. *Fable, Fact and History*. Philadelphia and New York: Chilton Co.—Book Division, 1957.

Trotsky, Leon. *The Russian Revolution*. Garden City, N.Y.: Doubleday & Co., 1959.

Truman, Harry S. *1945: Year of Decisions*. New York: New American Library, 1965.

————. *1946–1952: Years of Trial and Hope*. New York: New American Library, 1965.

Tugwell, Rexford G. *Off Course: From Truman to Nixon*. New York and Washington: Praeger Publishers, 1971.

Twain, Mark. *Innocents Abroad*. New York and Toronto: New American Library, 1966.

*Unterberger, Betty Miller. *America's Siberian Expedition, 1918–1920*. Durham, N.C.: Duke University Press, 1956.

USSR–USA: Cooperation for Mutual Benefit. Moscow: Novosti Press Agency Publishing House, 1973.

Waitley, Douglas. *The War Makers*. Washington and New York: Robert B. Luce, 1971.

*Walton, Richard J. *Cold War and Counter-Revolution*. New York: Viking Press, 1972.

Wehle, Louis B. *Hidden Threads of History*. New York: The Macmillan Company, 1953.

*Weintal, Edward, and Bartlett, Charles. *Facing the Brink*. New York: Charles Scribner's Sons, 1967.

Werstein, Irving. *The Cruel Years*. New York: Julian Messner, 1969.

Werth, Alexander. *Russia at War*. New York: Avon Books, 1964.

*Williams, William A. *American Russian Relations 1781–1947.* New York and Toronto: Rinehart & Co., 1952.

Winter, Ella. *And Not to Yield.* New York: Harcourt, Brace & World, 1963.

Winter, Ella, and Shapiro, Herbert, eds. *The World of Lincoln Steffens.* New York: Hill & Wang, 1962.

Wise, David, and Ross, Thomas B. *The Invisible Government.* Toronto, New York, and London: Bantam Books, 1964.

Woldman, Albert A. *Lincoln and the Russians.* Cleveland and New York: World Publishing Company, 1952.

Wolfe, Bertram D. *Communist Totalitarianism.* Boston: Beacon Press, 1956.

Woods, John A. *Roosevelt and Modern America.* New York: Collier Books, 1962.

Woytinsky, W. S. *Stormy Passage.* New York: Vanguard Press, 1961.

Wreszin, Michael. *Oswald Garrison Villard.* Bloomington, Ind.: Indiana University Press, 1965.

Zacharias, Ellis M. *Behind Closed Doors: The Secret History of the Cold War.* New York: G. P. Putnam's Sons, 1950.

Also consulted were issues of the *Atlantic Monthly,* the *Boston Globe, The Center Magazine, Foreign Affairs, Mankind, McCall's, Ms, The Nation, Nation's Business, Newsweek, New York Sunday News, The New York Times, The New York Times Magazine, The Palimpsest, The Reporter, Reprints from the Soviet Press, Saturday Evening Post, Soviet Life, Time, U.S. News & World Report, Variety,* and *Vital Speeches of the Day.*

INDEX

Index

Hammer, Armand, 68–70, 73, 75, 76, 173, 181, 194
Harding, Warren, 67, 70, 75, 79
Harriman, W. Averell, 115–117, 124, 152, 154
Hartmann, Leo, 37
Hay, John, 40
Hayter, William, 10
Haywood, Big Bill, 66
Herter, Christian, 144
Hillman, Sidney, 72
Hindus, Maurice, 84
Hitler, Adolph, 96, 97, 99, 102–106, 108–110, 114, 120, 193
Ho Chi Minh, 156, 162
Holmes, John Haynes, 85, 93
Holy Alliance, 19, 20, 24
Hook, Sidney, 81
Hoover, Herbert, 70–72, 82, 86, 87, 90
Hoover, J. Edgar, 66
Hopkins, Harry L., 105, 106, 114, 122
"hot line," 161, 164, 165
Howard, Roy, 91, 98
Hughes, Charles Evans, 70, 73, 75
Hull, Cordell, 91, 93, 98, 103
Hungary, 140

Ilin, M., 89
Ilf and Petrov (authors of *Little Golden America*), 95
India, 135
industrialization, Russian, 42, 67, 68, 72–75, 77, 82–84, 86, 89, 90
Industrial Workers of the World, 53, 54, 58, 66, 181
Intourist, 87
"iron curtain" speech, 129

Israel, 187–190
Italy, 98, 99, 109, 115, 126

Jackson, Andrew, 21, 22
Jackson, Henry, 187, 188, 190, 191, 195, 196
Japan, 41, 42, 57, 58, 90, 91, 93, 100, 101, 110, 114, 115, 122, 123, 125, 127
Jefferson, Thomas, 16–18, 27
Jews, 36–38, 40, 42, 43, 48, 85, 187, 189, 190, 191, 196
Johnson, Andrew, 35
Johnson, Hiram, 62
Johnson, Lyndon B., 135, 141, 147, 154, 159, 162–167
Johnston, Eric, 83, 111, 112
Jones, John Paul, 15, 16
Judson, William, 52

Kalinin, Mikhail, 101
Kamenev, Leo, 72
Kennan, George (surveyor), 38, 39, 42
Kennan, George F. (diplomat), 131, 132, 134, 135, 143, 154, 193, 196
Kennedy, John F., 101, 152–157, 159–162, 193
Kennedy, Joseph, 102
Kennedy, Robert, 160
Kerensky Revolution, 45–48, 50, 51, 53, 61, 73
Khrushchev, Nikita, 88, 98, 109, 123, 138–140, 142–162
Kissinger, Henry, 169, 170, 172, 191, 195
"kitchen debate," 145, 146
Kolchak, Alexander, 57, 60, 62, 64, 65
Konstantin, Grand Duke, 26